Communica
from
Heartstar

By the same author of
Being Loving is Being Healthy

Communications from Heartstar

through
Paul Lambillion

L.N. Fowler & Co. Ltd.
1201 High Road
Chadwell Heath
Romford
Essex RM6 4DH
England

ISBN 0 85243 795 1

Cover design by Michelle Thompson

First published in 1993 in the United Kingdom by
L. N. Fowler and Company Limited
for
Heartstar

Typeset in Times New Roman, 11/12 point
Printed and bound by Bell & Bain Limited, Glasgow.

Contents

INTRODUCTION

"COMMUNICATIONS FROM HEARTSTAR" & The W.F. Readings

In early 1985, whilst attending a week's course and retreat, I was allocated a session of counselling and spiritual assessment with a course leader. To my surprise, the gentleman, who was a remarkable and much respected sensitive and clairvoyant, suggested that in much of my work as a healer, I was in a very deep, altered state of consciousness akin to trance. It was further suggested that I should encourage this state to unfold much more as it would open a most significant doorway in my work as a spiritual teacher.

My immediate reaction was one of dismissal, for I have watched many trance or channelling sessions where the lecture or information was being provided by someone considered to be in such an altered state and I was not impressed by any of them. Many seemed to be a delusion of one kind or another, however honestly undertaken, and they rarely offered any teaching that would justify the theatrical displays usually accompanying such activities.

Some weeks later I stirred rather suddenly and very early from my night's sleep with the feeling that someone or something had woken me. As the rest of the family were still sleeping I went downstairs to make a drink and sat quietly looking out at the early morning light rising over the tree tops. I was soon overwhelmed by a warm feeling of deep humility and love. I was being hugged and embraced by all those things in life that are good, beautiful and inspiring. My thoughts were suddenly and quickly connected to that interview and I knew what I had been told was true and right. However much I didn't understand now I knew beyond any doubt that I must begin to develop the process of attunement necessary for some link or connection with God and His 'Angels' to be unfolded.

I began to meditate and seek attunement each week with a few friends in a prayer and meditation group dedicating the evening to the Highest Good and Divine Principle and always commencing the session with a recital of the Lord's Prayer. As time went by, memories of childhood experiences long suppressed yet relevant to this new pathway began to surface from the depths of my mind.

Eventually the first written and then verbal communication took place and it became clear to me that I was indeed privileged to be a channel for thoughts and ideas from a very beautiful and evolved level of consciousness.

Over the years the communications have grown, bringing teaching and wisdom that is both an inspiration and a creative challenge for those of us truly seeking to follow the spiritual path. From the earliest of words given the Source of the communications is identified as the exalted consciousness the Melchizedek within whose light and mind the link is granted. All the teachings are based upon an understanding of the most powerful revelation of God to humanity so far, being through The Christ, exemplified in the life of the Master and Initiate Jesus.

Over the years a considerable volume of information has been channelled and recorded and although the home group meetings have inevitably become a little less frequent, largely due to my busy teaching schedule, the volume of text continues to grow through the selected public communications given each year and also in the private interviews or readings that are now given regularly.

More recently I find that I am able to link with the source in almost normal consciousness to channel information and ideas. This is confirmation of a prediction made to me a couple of years ago.

The readings are proving to be enlightening and rewarding and sometimes challenging for an increasing number of seekers world-wide.

Whilst the readings and texts are always very cautious as to prognostications and always insist that our freedom of choice is inviolate, there have been some interesting insights offered, including the timing of Mrs Thatcher's departure as UK Prime

Minister suggested over a year beforehand when her position looked most secure and reiterated three weeks before she suddenly resigned. There has also been some interesting guidance, in one case solving the mystery as to the disease that was causing a high mortality rate amongst a herd of pigs!

Hitherto, some unedited transcripts have been circulated on a small scale to those who have requested them. I have also been able to share the ideas with others in a few of my workshops and study days. However, as the requests for copies grew, it was felt that the time had come for an organised publication of some of the communicated material. Hence the appearance of this little book — and the fulfilment of another prophesy!

The process of sifting through the large volume of information is a long and arduous one, some of the transcripts dealing with several topics at the same time. But the hard work of some loyal friends, especially, in the early days, Renate Roberts who has worked ceaselessly since the very beginning, recording and typing every word of the home sessions will ensure that before too long many others will benefit from the inspiration and wisdom of the Heart Star or 'W.F.' material.

And who is 'W.F.'? And Heart Star?

Amused by the often florid and extravagant names of so many 'Higher' sources of spiritual teachings, my sense of humour rather got the better of me when pressed to reveal the name of the mysterious 'source' who communicated every Wednesday evening in the lounge of my home. I came up with 'White Ferret' and amongst my friends the name has stuck to this day.

'Heart Star' refers to the Star of Twelve points which is the signature or symbol given by the source of the readings and which was independently dowsed in the ethers around my home town Bury St. Edmunds shortly after the communications commenced.

This volume contains some material received during the summer of 1991 and extracts from other readings and public sessions, including the answers to questions asked. I have endeavoured to edit and link the material as effectively as I could, with as little comment from me as possible. However, it is not only the words themselves that are significant but the energy, wisdom and love with which they are imbued by the White Brotherhood, that the reader may discern.

It is hoped that it will bring to you some inspiration and fresh insights to you as you make your way along the path of self-discovery and enlightenment in these exciting times.

May the love of God, and the light of the Christ always bless you.

Paul Lambillion
Bury St. Edmunds   Summer 1993
Suffolk UK

A Prayer

"Let all men discover the truth of themselves,
The power they have within their hearts.
Let all men know that the eye of God and the voice of the Father
Seeks always to open and express through them.
Let all men be conscious of the Light of their own hearts,
Let them see within themselves the power to transform,
The power to uplift and the love to heal.
Let all men see in the sky and the stars,
In the earth and in the waters of the sea,
The Love of the Christ within them.
Let all men be assured that when they are guided in their actions
and activities by the deepest urgings of their own hearts,
Then they are working with the True Light,
With the most open sphere of consciousness.
Let all men see from the goodness in their own hearts The Christ
within the hearts of all,
That they may be as one together,
Sharing the blissful union of such truth."

ONE

PLANES OF CONSCIOUSNESS AND BEING

There have been many references to planes of consciousness and levels of being in the communications. In this opening section are some fundamental ideas in relation to Man's overcoming of the planes of life within him from his earliest appearance upon the earth, experience in dream states and also in death.

20.7.88
"When in the early times Man was learning to work and to function upon earth, his primary role was to learn to blend the physical and the etheric or energistic natures of himself so that his earth body functions at its optimum level, enabling a true and clear flow of the forces from the etheric fields and bodies into the physical form. We refer to 'bodies' here because the etheric body is a complex vehicle composed of many levels and therefore it is perhaps wrong to speak of one body, but we will perhaps group them together and look at the combined or synthesised etheric human form.

This etheric body is an intricate web of force fields and energy patterns, having within it the potential to build and to hold together the physical form which Man needs and requires for incarnation. All the elements necessary for the construction of the human physical body by all the devic influences are blended through the energies of the etheric body.

The Solar energies, energies from your sun, flow along lines of force which cross and weave, throughout an individual etheric body and where these lines of force are flowing will be found the power and influence of the Cosmic Rays, the rays of Spiritual Fire and of course the vitality rays. This process is continuous, thus harmonising, synthesising, unifying and blending to produce the intelligence and energy necessary to structure Man's physical form.

Remember that the physical form is built by the devic intelligence and other angelic beings who work within the Will of the individual human entity and the pattern to which he has determined he shall live. They obey his genetic imagery, contained within his etheric Permanent or Great Atom.

This is the first aspect of Man's understanding of himself and the primary growth he must make is for secure control and fusion of his etheric and denser physical nature. When this has been satisfactorily attained we have to consider another level of Man's functioning, the level whereby the personality is revealed and perceived.

OVERCOMING THE ASTRAL/EMOTIONAL SELF

It is here that we see the emotions which colour your own perceptions and understanding of your thinking. It is through the Astral Man that the personality mostly functions. Those individual strengths and weaknesses which you recognise as the human 'you' are largely a manifestation of the Astral self. At this level we begin to perceive a man who is not simply animal, but a man of feeling, emotion and desire.

Therefore when the physical and energistic levels of Man have stabilised, Man must travel in consciousness through another realm , gaining a further mastery of himself, his personality, his feelings and it is here for most at the present time that the battle is being fought and the engagement with destructive aspects takes place — aspects that have been created within the Astral consciousness and the personality, and which are surfacing dramatically at this time. Powerful emotional forces are being exorcised and transmuted as Man wrestles with that which he has created within himself. The Astral consciousness is largely the consequence of destructive thought forms that Mankind has built and empowered since the Atlantean epoch and thus Man wrestles with his own created sphere of reality.

Indeed throughout the whole process of growth and initiation Man is battling with his own misunderstanding of that which he is: when a true understanding is gained and the personality mastered then we see a growth in strength the like of which has not been experienced before in this round of Human evolution. There comes forth an increase in confidence and personal esteem and an urge to be no longer the victim of the lower parts of one's emotional nature but to be identified with the higher aspects of self and the glorious Spirit hidden within.

THE MENTAL SELF

In the next stage of our growth we move from this level of development and consciousness to what we would call the lower Mental aspect of being.

Here concrete perceptions are found and the true Ego, that which understands the true path of the individual entity and which is connected to the soul begins to have greater sway over the functioning of an individual life. Thinking becomes clear and direct and Man truly begins to understand himself to see clearly that he is a being of immense light and power, with access to vast wisdom.

In this plane of his consciousness Man begins to understand his true nature: that he is a being who is built upon the powers and forces which come to him from the Mind of God. Man recognises that he is an individual aspect of the Divine and therefore has within him the Potential of the Divine albeit in a dormant state.

Furthermore we move through this lower concrete mind into the higher aspect of mind, the higher Mental self, which provides us with a more abstract area of self expression. It is an area which in terms of normal language cannot easily be described for here one becomes clear of emotions and increasingly oriented not just to a single individual ego but to the concept of the collective ego where one is bound inextricably to the lives and existence of others. On this plane Man knows himself to be at one with all things.

From here one moves to the planes of spiritual understanding and when Man's focus grows through the plane of the ego into the realms of the spirit and to be initiated truly into spiritual wisdom then of course Man begins to function with all the powers of the solar system and beyond. It is at the level of the spirit that Man begins to truly understand his connection with his Hierarchical grouping. He truly knows who he is and what he is. It is from this point that Man is able to focus upon his reality and to see it truly for what it is.

Thus the Personality of Man is essentially contained within his physical, etheric, Astral (emotional) selves, living and existing within these planes.

The Higher nature of Man, his Soul, is found in his higher mental self, his intuitive and spiritual realms.

Man truly experiences wholeness when he has consciously overcome all these planes within his being and integrated the lower and higher aspects into one dynamic, purposeful centre of wisdom and love.''

IN SLEEP

11.1.89

''As you are sleeping, your spirit leaves the physical realms and the focus of its consciousness will be upon the Astral level and therefore the Astral body also leaves the physical, encapsulating and taking the mental and spiritual layers of your being with it. It is only the physical and the etheric which will stay together, although some atoms of the Astral and mental bodies and some atoms of the spiritual bodies too will remain within the physical sphere. But the general movement is away from the physical to enable it to rest. Thus your consciousness is focused elsewhere and you will deal with circumstances as if you are in another world and another life for perhaps anything up to nine or ten hours. For you are in another realm of life while you sleep.

When this is completed and you have to make your return, then you come back into complete alignment and rapport with the physical body and this is done very simply and very easily.

The bodies are linked by a subtle cord and which pulsates gently. It can stretch so that it can be extremely long, and it is possible for you to be a long way from your physical home in three dimensional terms, during your period of sleep. As you come close to the physical on your return, so the cord will contract. This cord enables your mind to control the mechanisms

4

for respiration and for the beating of your heart so that there is a continual rhythm active at every moment to sustain the physical consciousness.

As you re-enter your body, you reach a state whereby your mind begins once more to associate with the physical realm and the memories attached to it. Gradually you remove yourself from the state known as sleep into an awakened, stimulating and enjoyable, we would hope, state of life.''

IN DEATH

5.4.89

''When your loved ones leave you and the physical life, they become more conscious of the spiritual dimension of their own selves and they begin to release the attachment to the physical and the etheric level of consciousness. They now start to focus more clearly upon the areas or planes of mind and the Astral world, particularly those where they can still be in tune with the feelings of the earth, those feelings which have been so dominant for so long.

Thus it is that you are able to communicate with them through human channels whose minds are attuned for that particular function. You must always remember here that it is possible for all souls who are upon the earth plane to receive impressions and indeed to benefit from the urgings and the loving guidance that is given from the other dimensions of life. All men are in a sense in communion with the lives and beings of those in the higher planes or the planes which interpenetrate your own world.

For many souls the period between incarnations is perhaps short and therefore they return more quickly to the earth, within a period of one to three or even four hundred of the earth years and it is possible sometimes for the return to be very quick indeed, depending on the individual karma and also the needs of the planet and humanity as a whole.

It is also important to remember that there are some souls who incarnate upon the earth because they choose to serve the Greater Good, although there is no requirement within the Laws of the Universe that they should do so and this is a wonderful and remarkable sacrifice to make. It is similar in some respects to the offering of itself by the Christ Being at the time of the Master Jesus.''

18.5.88

''When you move through the portal called death into the next reality or the next consciousness, you are the same, more enriched perhaps and free from some of the rules and constraints you adopted before, but in truth you have gone nowhere and you have left nothing. You have simply changed the way that you have oriented your thinking patterns and the focus of your mind has moved.

This is what we mean by the planes of reality. Life, Birth and Death are a shifting in focus of mind from one area or plane of truth to another, and so, when you think in terms of journeying through the planes, do not think of it in terms of an arduous physical endeavour, but rather as a movement in your thinking, a shifting of the position at which the sharp point of focus within your consciousness is re-directed and shown afresh another way of being, a new way of perceiving.

This is really the truth of the planes, the planes within the universe and within you.

You are in that part of reality which allows different aspects of you to experience different consciousness at different times, but in essence the central part of your consciousness is always able to dominate all others and therefore you will know that you are either focused in the physical world, the Astral worlds or worlds beyond. But you, you are a constant, because remember, within you at all times is the Spark of Eternity, and to the Spark of Eternity 'all that is' is within it, is permanent and forever. It is only the picture that it sees through the frames of life which alters, and therefore conditions its responses to what it sees. But the inner essence of you, the Infinite Spark of Life is permanent and is simply viewing all things in their place in their time.

You can exist in any plane, anywhere, at any time you chose.''

TWO

TIME AND ITS INFLUENCE

The nature and mystery of time has been discussed by the communicators on several occasions. Here are some of the insights they have sought to share.

28.11.89

''As Time uses its power and as the illusions begin to clear, thus will all men see the true patterns within their souls. For a new time is upon you, a new element of the Divine Kingdom is coming into the focus of Man's Mind and thus we see clearly Father that Thy Kingdom will come upon the earth as it is in Heaven.''

10.7.91

''We have spoken to you in the past on the subject of time and we have sought to explain how it is that you live upon the earth and experience your movement of consciousness. You Live and move in time and space and thus your experience is movement within that space. The speed at which this movement occurs determines the dynamic nature of the experience which is gained.

Man will realise that time, in earth terms, is really an attempt to explain his breadth of experience and to place experience in sequence with a beginning and an end, and you must understand that the need for time or the understanding of linear time grew as Man became immersed in the illusion of material things and three dimensional thinking. The more immersed one's consciousness is in the lowest physical vibration, which of course is what you would understand to be solidity and the realm of form, then the more it is necessary for Man to work and explore in a linear time sense.

As we move away from the earth, increasingly the nature of time begins to alter and this of course has been discovered as Man has been able to physically remove himself from the main gravitations, the electrical and etheric pull of the earth.

He has experienced planes of existence where time would not exist in the same manner and intensity that it does upon the earth. Only so long as one has a connection with the earth does your time exist, but as soon as that connection is severed then no longer does earth time, in its normal linear function, have any real meaning or influence upon thought or activity. A totally different set of parameters begin to be employed in the understanding of sequence and the way in which events and circumstances appear to form together into a cohesive whole upon which we can move our gaze from one point to another.

PAST AND FUTURE

We did explain to you also that in relation to time and the earth we have to seek to understand that which is professed to be past and future experience. From our understanding, the future and the past are in themselves illusory concepts, for the past and the future and all the variables which exist therein exist as much now as they do in their own space, and it is purely a question of how you direct your Will-Energy and concentration that determines where you are or appear to be in space and time.

To refer to an experience as a past life is somewhat an illusion for it can be better expressed as an alternative or complimentary experience.

This is very important to realise because this explains a significant truth, an important empowerment of human kind. It means that just as there are alternatives which you can attune to as your past experiences, so there are alternatives which you can attune to as your future experiences, for the past and the future, in Cosmic terms, are the same. There is no difference between the two and it is only the degree or the nature of experience which we have that determines where we place it in the time-frame of our consciousness.

There are many fanciful stories where it is suggested that it is possible for Man to travel through time and to go into the future and into the past.

It is perfectly possible for one who exists in the future to make a connection with the past and it is perfectly possible for one from the past to make a connection with that which appears to be in the future. This has been done. Therefore it would be possible for you here to experience an entity who has placed the focus of his consciousness in this time-frame, although for him, previous to his expression and appearance here, the main concentration and impetus of his consciousness was in that which for you would appear for you in the future.

THE FOCUS OF CONSCIOUSNESS

All those individuals who you understand and know as possibilities in the future exist as realities just as much as you do here in this moment of time. The entities which you consider the past equally exist now and could be imagined to function just as you do now.

If for example you were to choose a period in that which you refer to as history and into that particular period you place your focus and attention, you will begin to become increasingly imbued with the ideas of that life. Ultimately you will become attached to that period of experience and the more you draw energy through your consciousness to that time-frame and focus your light upon that idea, the more of your soul force there is in that experience. It would be easy for you to leave this reality and to move into another reality from the past and find yourself experiencing the past as you would experience the present.

It is equally possible for you to place your consciousness into the future and to be engaged with such intensity in activities which you would perceive as being of the future, that you would have more of your consciousness concentrated there than in the here and now. Then you would be engaged in a future activity but it would be happening now.

This is quite a conundrum for you to consider but you must also then apply to this truth the following and equally interesting idea that as a creature you exist at many levels and in many dimensions of self and that there are other parts or aspects of you. These parts of you are living other lives and are in other realities

9

now and equally you could encounter a part of yourself in another reality should you take the choice to make such a journey. These other parts of yourself in other realities sometimes come very close to you as you grow, progress and live.

This is why it is possible, in a fleeting moment, that you can suddenly feel very drawn to either a life which you would understand to exist in your history or a life which seems to you to be fantastic and beyond the normal realms of possibility. It is because a part of your consciousness is active there and it is making this reality known to you almost like a whisper in the deep chambers of your mind and your heart.

Remember also that as we look at this current phase of awareness, the ultimate decade of this two thousand year cycle, you will find that there is a particular funnel of activity and possibility through which the consciousness of humanity is being drawn. Whilst you are focused in this reality now, you will find that the strands of possibility to which your consciousness is attracted, are being drawn closer together and this is being done by the planetary Masters and the Hierarchies.

By their will, in tune with the Divine Plan, they are weaving all the strands of possibility through a small but clearly defined opening or doorway and as these strands are drawn together they are pulled through and out into an even greater area of possibility, expression and consciousness.

This is why the sun, the light which you can see as the sun, is shedding some of the most powerful, most stirring and yet inspiring energies and rays which Man has ever experienced. All that holds Man in bondage to time and limitation is his unwillingness to believe in himself as a transcendent being, beyond time and space.''

RELATIVE TIME AND QUICKENING

16.8.89

''Time is a relative idea. The existence and nature of time depends on where you are. Consider how the understanding of time upon your own planet has changed for a Man who existed in times long ago on your earth where there was no technology as you would understand it and where there was only the rising of the sun and the coming of the moon in the darkened sky for him to determine the changes from one period to another. Where there was the clear demarcation of seasonal change for him in certain parts of the planet he was able to understand the rhythms and cycles of life and within that framework he began to unfold his relationship to all experience through this mapping of time.

Within your society there is now an ability to look at time from an abstract point of view and to determine how time should work, but even within the context of your own planet you have to have dual standards in terms of time, for you have to adjust when you move around the earth from one earth time zone to another, for time is a very local concept even upon the earth.

Thus it is that when you move around the earth you begin to see time for the illusion that it truly is and so you must understand that which you would call time, the distance between two events, is becoming shorter. Or should we say as Man's consciousness is rising, more seems to be occurring in time, there appears to be a quickening of events and circumstances and hence life, for many people, has become a crowded and even cluttered experience.

This is because, as you have been told before, you are in the pangs of birth of a new experience of consciousness and just as the mother's breath quickens when she is giving birth to the child, so it is that the constituent rhythms of consciousness quicken as the birth of a New Consciousness approaches.

Thus time appears to quicken and Man must work within that time to quicken his own consciousness so that the relative experience for him is constant.

Where Man is evolving slowly and he is resistant to change then his experience of time may be very difficult, for he will seem to involve himself in a spinning and uncontrollable whirl of activity. But where a man has learned to attune through his soul to the greater powers of the Universe within him, then as time quickens it will be as for nothing with him. For his own consciousness will adjust and begin to see that time for him is merely a temporary experience of rationality and he has no longer any need of it.

TIMELESSNESS

If you wish to think of timelessness we suggest you think of those moments where, when you are sitting quietly, you begin to lose contact with thinking or perceiving, where your senses are not being bombarded by those words or pictures, ideas or sounds which normally seek to govern your busy world and dominate your attention; where you are able to sit and allow your mind to drift, to day-dream, only to return realising that a period had elapsed where there was no particular focus or activity for you upon the physical world.

Thus it is that you begin to experience the timelessness of reality and through meditations expand your access to timelessness. This is also why it is in some respects, apparently possible to change the impossible, for through the timelessness of the Divine you can bring any slot of experience through into your reality if it would serve the best creative purpose of the individual and the collective whole.

BEING A MASTER OF TIME

And so, in your understanding of time, always perceive yourself to be in control of time. Recognise that you are given time as a method of understanding and measuring your experience. If this paradigm is no longer working to your advantage and appears to place undesirable limits upon you then remember that you are the master or the controller of your experience of time and you can begin to alter your perception of things sufficiently to give yourself adequate space and opportunity to accomplish all that you need to in your life.

Time does not exist when Man moves from the limitations of his small world and when he goes into the greater world and the universe. As your physics have discovered, there is no time, there is only life and the moment of consciousness which exists for you now. Time is purely an illusion to secure you within the experience of the physical world.''

THE QUICKENING OF TIME AND THE SEASONS

14.8.91

''You will notice in your affairs that even time itself will appear to be moving more quickly. This is true, for the vibrations of the earth and all the phenomena which are associated with the earth are quickening. This can be likened to any birth where there is a quickening in the metabolism of the mother as she begins to prepare for that last and most beautiful urging of the new life into its existence and birth.

And here there is a quickening of the breath, of the breath of life itself. This quickening is with all Mankind now. It is with you all here and thus your time will appear to move more quickly. Your daily affairs will seem to be charged often with an urgency and even a fleeting quality which makes all things difficult to hold on to. Even in nature you will see this quickening occur within the plants, the trees and the creatures of the earth. Their own cycles of activity are quickening. Within your seasons you will see the changes as if you move into the Autumn before its normal time has come. Even the Winter may appear sometimes to come suddenly and quickly and the Spring will follow often more quickly than you would have imagined possible. The seasonal changes for many will be less clearly defined.''

THE ILLUSION, NOW, AND EMPOWERMENT

26.6.91

''We often refer to times past. We refer to incarnations which we can understand or which we can express to you best within the framework of past lives. But there is no past and no future.

Those lives which appear to be past lives could equally be considered lives which are happening now or lives which are occurring in some future space and in a sense they are casting their shadow back across this life and this reality.

It is important for you to recognise that as a being you are a multi-dimensional creature and the soul places many aspects of itself within consciousness at all times. These planes of consciousness are divergent although they do in fact interweave very closely and it is possible for you to consider your past incarnations in the sense that they are happening now and that those events which allude to the past are still unfolding.

The significance of this understanding is crucial to the total unfolding of your awareness for it tends to support the truth that the only important point in your life is the moment in which you find yourself thinking now and that there is no other phase in your experience which is of greater importance whatsoever. It is this moment, this reality which has the power, the true power, and from your point of view it means that you can, if you like, change your reality and build a reality in keeping with whichever consciousness you may choose. You can build a reality that can obliterate one of the futures which you have already constructed. You can then form another future which you would find more acceptable and more in tune with the flow of your current thinking.

THE SOUL SEES MANY OPTIONS

You can imagine, it is rather as if you were in the centre of a large board, a game-board which is covered with many lines of progression and as you move out from the centre of this board so you begin to follow a certain option within the pattern. But to keep the whole pattern alive although your main focus may be along one of the lines of the pattern, you are really looking at this pattern from above as would the soul. Thus you are also conscious of the other paths, the other options upon the board. Your soul consciousness is following those equally as much as that one which you, the personality, are following now.

When you choose to make an alteration in your pattern you can shift the focus of your consciousness from one lane of reality into another and all that is changing is the focus, the dominance of your attention. But, at the same time, all the other paths on the board exist and they are all real for you. From the point of your own higher observation you can see and understand them clearly and you can move from one to the other as you would so choose.

Now this board upon which you are moving is not flat. It is not two-dimensional. It is multi-dimensional and not only can

14

you move from side to side but you can move backwards and forwards, up and down and in any direction you choose. Therefore you are blessed with many options and it may be that as you move along one of your options, through the higher vision of your soul, you can recall experiences contained within a different choice which another part of you is able to understand.

This is true for all men, for all entities and thus you can link with different realities within your own experience and understand lives of expression and alternative realities and see them as being in the past. But it is just as easy to consider that they are in the future for from our point of view the patterns for the future are already there, they already exist upon life's game-board.

TIME AND HEALTH

This understanding is so valuable and liberating. Let us consider this from the point of view of your physical home, your physical body. If at any time you have experienced physical wholeness or health, you have experienced a sense of completeness within the physical self, and if you have experienced that once, then it is perfectly possible for you to experience it again as often and for as long as you wish. This means that you can be healthy as often and for as long as you choose to be.

It is a question of you learning to suspend the limitations of your thinking thus far and to place within your focus the ideas of completeness, the concept of wholeness, of health and your being attuned so that truth of wholeness within you which you have experienced in the past, you can experience in the future. In such a mode you overcome the constraints of time and elect to experience the Now of your choosing.''

THREE

OF PLANETS, SPACEMEN AND SPACE CRAFT

This section presents some of the communications that refer to our place in the Cosmos and those other Entities also living within the three dimensional Universe who come close to us on Earth at times.

13.1.88

"Man, through his personality, finds it very difficult to understand that his own life form is just one of many types of experience. He himself has touched many levels of reality which are considerably different from the one that he now works and lives within. Therefore he will find it equally difficult to understand and relate to life in another time and another place, in a dimension which can interact and interpenetrate that which he uses now but in such a fashion that he cannot sense it or know it with a physical perception.

There are many rumours about those souls (astronauts) who have left your earth and its influence to touch the areas of space and to move nearer to your moon. Indeed, some have walked upon the surface of your moon. They have said that they saw no life there. They have said that as far as they were concerned the moon is a dead experience, consisting mainly of certain minerals and lower vibrational forms of substance which, though interesting, are of no great report.

Every action of those who were astronauts at the present time is monitored very closely by those who are no longer living within the sphere of the earth and also by those who have never been here, for it is not possible to allow the erring ways of Man to wander out into the vast areas of space and universal influence, unattended and unaided. Not only could he do damage to himself,

16

but more importantly, of course, he could do damage to those he does not see and does not understand.

Therefore, all of these works are governed and aided, for we wish to see success in Man's understanding of his environment, both the immediate one and that into which he reaches, in hope and in a wish to become greater in his knowledge and in his wisdom. Do remember though that all of these things are seen from a limited viewpoint.

When you talk of travelling through space, you inevitably do so from the viewpoint of your own concept of time and you begin to calculate how long it will take for you to reach the nearest planet and then how long it will take you to reach the nearest star, and so on. All of your reactions to the viability of such an enterprise are governed by your very limited understanding of the physical roles of the reality in which you live.

LIFE ON OTHER PLANETS

First of all, each of the planets in your solar system is inhabited by intelligent life forms. There is none that is not .

There are entities from other planets who come to the earth. Entities who seek to be here, to watch and to come, not in the form of the spirit as you would understand it, but who will manifest through the same (physical) dimension you are in now, simply at a slightly altered tone or higher frequency . To come close to the earth, they adopt the form of a craft or some kind of moving and controllable vehicle which they can use enabling them to come close to the vibrations of the lower ethers and the physical dimension of the planet.

It is also possible for you, between incarnations, to use certain of the vibrations of the planetary systems, to attach yourselves to them and to grow with them and benefit from them. This is why you have sometimes a particular interest in a certain planet and you will begin to find your mind wandering to that place and wondering what it is that attracts you so.

There are also life forms connected with some of the other planets in this solar pattern which you would not be able to understand easily. The terms of reference for their existence tend to be completely alien to you. Their view of reality is totally different to yours and therefore the common ground which is necessary for communication between you would not exist. You would find them almost unattainable in terms of understanding and intellectual rapport.

It is not because they are hostile any more than you would be hostile. It is simply because there is, as yet, no simple link between you and them at the conscious level. There is of course, the Divine Essence within them as there is within you and this is always there, but because of your level and period of growth you are not able, at the present time, to relate to these souls and to what they seek to do or their own way of being.

Upon the other planets within your system there are some souls who might be considered more highly evolved than Man is himself in that they have not strayed or rebelled from their pattern within the Divine Principle at any time. They are therefore more in tune and in touch with that Divine Principle and are able to relate to it more clearly. However, because of this, they have not been able to experience some of the more exacting parts of the lives that you have in the physical world and so, in other respects, they could be considered to be not so evolved.

Your lives and your world is really an illustration of how the Divine can begin to redeem and transmute that which has distorted and lost its way, into something more beautiful, as it returns back to its home in consciousness. From an apparent disaster, the Divine, the Father, turns in yet another triumph. For from His child who sank so low, He will ultimately produce His finest jewel and this is the height to which Mankind must climb as he leaves behind the desperate times and moves back to the light and to the illumination of pure thought and pure being.''

EXTRA-TERRESTRIALS AND MAN

1.6.88

''Many of you will know it is often vehemently denied that there has ever been any recorded connection with what you would understand to be those of extra-terrestrial origin. That is not the case. It is a very common occurrence. Also bear in mind that each one of you here is also an extra-terrestrial, temporarily involved in earth consciousness, and therefore it is merely a matter of time before the illusion which is keeping this information from Mankind is pulled away and the truth is revealed to everyone."

24.7.91

"It may well be during the next few years, especially during the next five to seven, the reported sightings of beings who are not of this earth, beings in whom the humanity is expressed in rather a different way to your own may be observed more frequently in and around your life here on earth. The reports of crafts, of ships and of vehicles which weave an interplanetary and interstellar path are possibly likely to be on the increase. Now many of these beings, even where they use a thought form which is a vehicle, will use it at such a frequency that when they come to the earth the vehicle will not be seen. It will be resonating at a tonal level or frequency which will allow it to exist in the ethers but not within the lower dimensions of the physical world.

If we look at this in yet another manner, you will understand that although these vehicles are working in the tones of the ethers they may, from time to time, leave impressions in the ethers which are so powerful that ultimately they will become visible on the earth. There are many reports of marks which are unexplained on the earth, in various crops, on plateau and so on, and sometimes, it is indicative of a specific level of communication and contact has been made in the ethers and as the ethers have quickened the physical level, then the expression has become clear and visible in physical human and earth terms and so you will see some phenomena.

We are not here seeking to explain the corn circles, as you call them, for they exist for many different reasons, but some unusual phenomena proliferating at this time are the visual evidence of a specific exchange of Divine energy which comes from the Solar Logos.

This energy creates a particular funnelling or force above each of these areas and fields which in turn alters the patterns in the ethers around them. This in due course feeds energy into the earth which the earth can absorb and so assist in the raising of the planetary vibrational field and consciousness .

There are many beings from other planets and from other solar systems and indeed even further than your own particular galaxy who come at this time to observe and support the earth.

BEINGS WHO WATCH THE EARTH

If you were to take your mind beyond this planet and through your own solar system, there will be beings who are watching the earth now. These beings are here to observe, not to interfere, but perhaps to assist where opportunity may arise, in the perfect unfoldment of the new awareness for the planet. There are beings whose consciousness and therefore whose vehicles are based beyond the solar system but are found close by and they are also around the earth, around your system, trying to support the activity and the quickening of the vibration which is now in manifestation.

As we are here with you now there are beings from other planes and other planets who are watching us and they are observing the way in which some, if but a few, of the creatures of the earth are seeking to listen to information which comes from beyond this earth, and for them it is a puzzle. It is a puzzle as to why more of Mankind are not willing to listen to the thoughts and ideas of other levels. You would derive great benefit from many of the insights and understandings which they could share with you if you were prepared to attune to and listen to them. They could teach you ways upon the earth which would be remarkable, for whilst they are not creatures of the earth they have experienced conditions which are very similar and they are still living in a stage which is very much like the ethers of this planet. Therefore they can understand solidity, the world of form, intense density and the laws which govern physical manifestation in a way which is difficult for you to grasp.

You may find that in the weeks and months to come there may be some more frequent claim of extra-terrestrials. Of course some of these will inevitably be hoaxes, some of them will be preposterous in the claims and the suggestions which they make.

For no being which has the power and the resource to come close to the earth would be bothered to use his energies and time upon some of the trivial and rather ridiculous claims and suggestions which are made in some of the stories which you may hear from time to time. But there are beings who come close to the earth who will make contact with you if you wish them to and they understand the Great Design.

EXTRA-TERRESTRIAL ASSISTANCE

One of their missions at the moment is to assist in rectifying some of the ecological and environmental damage which has been wrought by humanity. They are especially active around the poles of the earth in seeking to bring chemical influence of a kind which may assist in the structural retention of the layers of the ozone and other important and valuable elements around the earth itself. They are also trying to bring light and energies of diffusion which may help humanity cope with the intense brightness of the new light which will be experienced everywhere upon the earth in the next period of some twenty to thirty years.

You may notice that the light appears to be brighter. The light around the earth appears to be stronger and some of the extra-terrestrial beings are trying to bring webs of light which will refract and filter some of these energies for you as they come through into your sphere of normal life.

There are also beings who come from other levels who are seeking to work upon the earth itself and in the density of the earth. Some of the rectification is in connection with the myriad of tunnels which you have made in the earth's crust. Many of these tunnels have been made in the course of searching for apparently necessary fuels, such as oil and coal and so on. Some of these tunnels and holes in the earth, as you know, have been made in pursuit of luxurious items such as precious jewels and even precious metals.

Here there is difficulty facing them, for much of the damage is profound and the earth is irritated by it and the scars which it is experiencing in the skin and flesh of its own body. Some of the extra-terrestrial beings are helping in the restructuring of the

B

tissue which will support these particular intricate tunnels and webs which Man has made.

Others come close to you because they are from a similar planetary system to the one which is the one of your own origin. Therefore, as you have come from a particular star system, those who live upon the same star system and have learned to travel in a relatively physical dimension and retained their conscious link with their planetary and star source, come to assist you, to be around the earth now although they have never incarnated in an earth mental pattern and in an earth body as you have done here.

Understand that you are not simply planetary beings. Neither are you creatures of this solar system, but merely temporary residents here.

You are children of the Cosmos and all its splendour and wisdom is around you, supporting you, loving you.

Wonderful minds seek to link with you, so to bring to Mankind a fresh, deeper awareness of his Cosmic origin.

Be assured of that and rejoice that it is so."

FOUR

THIS RACIAL EPOCH ON EARTH —
LEMURIA AND ATLANTIS

The teachings have always recounted the idea of Man existing upon earth through earlier civilisations, civilisations in which Man was a more aware and hence gifted creature then he is now. And also that Man's true origins are to be found beyond this solar system. These extracts allude to those ideas.

SOULS INTO INDIVIDUALITY

7.11.90

"When Man was given his opportunity to leave the Source of his being and to differentiate into many experiences, the souls of humanity were cast off into life and into the whole of the created Cosmos. There was for all souls who were issued forth from the Divine the possibility to enjoy a width of experience which, in human terms, is impossible for us here to even begin to imagine.

Thus it was that all souls, at one moment, were cast forth into life, into reality so that God, the Source from which all come, could express Himself in an infinite number of possible ways and each human soul has within the complete and beautiful possibility of expressing God in the way he conducts his own experience and life."

20.11.91

''Man in himself does not understand the vastness of his reality. Most men have no conception of their heritage and the way in which they have grown. During the Lemurian consciousness Man began to adopt effectively his human form. Before that period there was no true connection between Man and his physical self as you now understand it. The first real human racial sojourn upon the earth was as a consequence of the unfoldment of the Lemurian race and its sub-races.

Prior to the Lemurian epoch there was a time when humanity had as its densest form what you would understand to be its emotional and desire nature. It had no more than that. This particular race was known as the 'Adamic' race which lived in an equivalent of the Astral plane, or Astral Consciousness and had no stable connection with the physical earth.

The 'Hyperborean' was the next grouping and the Hyperborean as it came close to the earth had an ability to work in the ethers or the subtle physical planes, but no more, and it was able to build an etheric form and exist as an etheric being."

7.10.90

"Thus it was that many beings came close and into the influence of the earth and its gravitational forces and as these entities partook of the experience of the physical dimension they none-theless were very much aware of their spiritual nature. They were still very much in contact with the Source from which they had come and knowing of their true identity. It is rather as if they were able to sample the earth in a very light and simple form without becoming totally immersed and controlled by the physical as you tend to be here now. They were able to live a life which was imbued with the love of the Divine Being, a life which was initially a joy and a paradise.

At this time Man was a complete being in the sense that he was an androgyne. He was both male and female at once, a complete entity. This was the beginning of time upon the earth. These were the early days. These were the experiences of the first Man of your race.

As time progressed and experience unfolded, the inquisitive nature which was growing within the soul body of Man began to wish to push further and further, deeper and deeper into the physical experience and as this occurred there was a very gradual, but nonetheless real distancing from the Essence of the Being from which he had come and so he had to work more steadily at maintaining his at-onement with the Divine Being.

Very often during this period Man would be able to choose

clearly the way in which his life would unfold. He could decide when he would be born and when he would withdraw from the earth experience and an incarnation could be for terms of time, many, many hundreds of earth years. Thus it was that death had no power over Man whatsoever as it does today, for Man was aware that he had the freedom to come and to go from this plane as he chose to do.

This first experience upon the earth was a joyful one. The first continent upon which Man experienced was the one known as Lemuria. This was the first experience of the soul entity entering the consciousness of the earth physical form, but it was a very light connection indeed and the early physical bodies were made purely of light ethers and did not have the dense physical substances which you have within your frames now.

As time progressed so the bodies became more and more dense and heavy and Man became immersed within the earth experience."

DEVELOPING PHYSICAL FORM

19.9.90

"Through the progression of Lemuria in its earliest times, the most appropriate forms of the human physique began to take a more stable shape. In the earlier times the physical form which was being evolved and developed was prone to very rapid changes in its structure. It was highly unstable and it was one in which no kind of long-term existence could have been enjoyed, for within seconds of your time, very often, the form would change and it would change very significantly, so that within minutes or hours the form would scarcely be recognisable in relation to its original structure.

Even in the so-called adult form which was developed one would see an instability which would make it extremely difficult for the entity to become as one with his densest physical body. He would have eventually built a form which in the ethers were good and fairly stable, but the physical form to which he was connected took many aeons of time to become the more permanent and effective structure which we are inclined to think of today.

It is very similar, in certain respects, to the way in which the soul through its lower bodies makes an attachment to the physical form whilst in its embryonic state prior to birth. The connection is there, but it is far from permanent.

Of course the link was meant to be one of convenience and experience, the inhabiting of a physical mantle in which experience could be gained and it was possible for Man, through the lower energies which he was able to touch in the physical form, those energies which link with the Animal and Vegetable Kingdoms and of course the Mineral Kingdom itself, to draw upon the animal nature of matter and to use that consciousness to ground himself, bringing him into full companionship with the planet upon which he was incarnating.

It acted rather like a magnet to enable him to walk the earth, just as in the same way those who tread upon other planets where there is no gravitational pull, need, whilst they are still in the physical form, some form of magnetism to help retain their link with that other planet.

At that time the same was true for Man and he needed the physical link with the earth to be sustained, and there was a tendency for the early Man of this period to leave the earth very spontaneously and of course consciously. There was a conscious exchange from one level of reality to another.

You must understand here that, in certain respects, individual consciousness had not grown or evolved as much as your consciousness has now and so the exchange, whilst it was one in which the human being was aware of what was occurring, was nonetheless occurring at a much lower level of sensitivity than would be the case today. It was relatively easy for the early Lemurian creature to move in and out of his physical form.

However, as time passed he became rather attached to his physical from and thus the beginning of the almost obsessive link with physical reality began to come into effect.

ENTHRALMENT AND SEXUALITY

The embryonic desire nature of Lemurian Man began the process of enthralment with the physical realms and he became almost obsessed with the animal like quality of his nature. There were many abuses of this particular ability which he discovered. Some of these abuses especially linked with the aspects of procreation and the way in which, in the physical terms, the concept of the 'triune' nature of life was celebrated by the coming together of two elements of being, that of the Father and Mother aspect producing the Son, in the third and most beautiful celebration of the two polarities of life unified.

It is during the Lemurian period that this particular point of obstruction began to take on a very forceful place within the consciousness of humankind and Man became obsessed with his sexuality and with the need to express sexual energy, either in the dominance of the male form or the dominance of the female form, either in the nature of the one who showed a greater manifestation of the male aspect of the Divine Being or of the female aspect of the Divine Creature.

In due course this was the precipitation of the bringing forth of a man who was a part of the Being and not a completeness of the Being. If you like, it was the period which heralded the disappearance of the androgyne creature to be replaced by the one who displayed a singularity of sexuality, either a predominance of maleness or a predominance of femaleness.

As time passed within this development of consciousness Man began to find increasing difficulty in leaving the physical dimension. The magnetic attraction of the physical began to overwhelm the lower aspects of Man's consciousness and the movement from one level to another and back became increasingly difficult. Man even began to forget his true essence and his real connection with the higher levels and thus the beginnings of the separation from his Divine nature took place. Man became increasingly outer-directed in his thinking.

There was a time during the Lemurian epoch when Man could quite easily enjoy an incarnation upon the earth which would have been far greater than the life span which you currently enjoy. In the early times the physical incarnation of the spiritual Man was very short, lasting perhaps only for days, weeks or months. Eventually it became years and from years into decades and so on and Man became a creature who would move easily into the earth-life and yet retain his Divine awareness so that there was a continuous infusion of spiritual power into his being."

BIRTH AND DEATH

7.11.90

"Very often at this time Man would be able to choose consciously the way in which his life would unfold. He would decide when he would be born and when he would withdraw from the earth experience, and this could be, in terms of time, many, many hundreds of earth years.

Thus it was that death had no power over Man whatsoever, as it does today, for Man was aware that he had the freedom to come and to go as he would choose to do. In a sense this is still the reality but Man no longer believes that this is so and because of his belief pattern, or should we say unbelief, he is trapped within the bounds of his own limiting consciousness and awareness and with the karmic patterns which he has unfolded throughout aeons of time.

As he became engrossed with the consciousness of the physical and some of the perversions which were to take place, Man began to lose this ease of access to the higher vibrations and the power with which they endow him. Increasingly, he lost the central and most beautiful element of his heritage and he commenced the descent into a consciousness of separation, limitation and despair.

Even so, through much of the time of the first period of Man's evolution and experience upon the earth in Lemuria, Man grew and became a beautiful being, one who in the main was still in tune with his Divine Essence and his Being.

The Lemurian race lived in the Pacific region, and was able eventually to build a body of physical matter and to come completely into earth existence. In due course, through various possibilities in existence Man's experience became corrupted and the civilisation of Lemuria was eventually to disappear. As the earth changed the way in which it functioned in relation to the Solar Body, so it was that it's axis also altered its relative position, and the seas moved and the earth changed. There were volcanic disturbances, and the Lemurian being was eventually scattered across the earth as all his homeland gradually disappeared beneath the seas."

ATLANTIS

6.11.90

"There was another great race of Man which was also lost to us, a race in which Man achieved the heights of his experience and an understanding of the sciences and laws of physics.
The roots of this race came from the Lemurians who settled upon Atlantis, with other extra-terrestrial influences.

In the Atlantean period Man became a very selfish creature, a creature who was very war-like; one who was extremely acquisitive and who would seek to control and impose; one who believed in self above all things. Thus it was that over a period of time the corrupt Man that lived upon the earth was moved and shaken, and as you well know through your own history and your religions, once again great changes came upon the earth.

It is also the case that Atlantis disappeared beneath the sea and this occurred in two particular phases.

The first phase was many aeons ago, something in the region of twenty-four thousand years, when the first portion of Atlantis disappeared and this, as a matter of interest, is the period which is mentioned in the Biblical flood, that in which Noah and his family were seen to be removed from one area to another.

There was further movement of the earth during the latter period of the Civilisation of Atlantis and this final disappearance occurred somewhat in the region of twelve thousand years ago when the remainder of Atlantis gradually disappeared beneath the area of the Atlantic Ocean. Then there were to be just a few remnants of that Civilisation upon earth.

If we were to look to the end of the period of Atlantis many thousands of years ago, the remnants of that civilisation, in physical terms, are still with you now in parts of North and Central America, within the Middle East and even regions of India and beyond in the subcontinents of Asia.

There is that part of Ireland, off the coast of this country,

England, and areas of the north west of England up along the coast of Scotland and into the islands of the sea. These are all lands which were in some respects associated with the fringes of the Continent of Atlantis and still contain some of its physical vibration.

Some aspects also of the Caribbean which were associated with Atlantis, areas off the east coast of the Americas, and much of the area which is now the Atlantic Ocean was once above the surface of the waters. At its inception, it was a wonderful and very powerful civilisation which was geared to the understanding of the scientific nature of life and the way in which knowledge could be used.

Unfortunately, because of the cruelty, arrogance and also the acquisitiveness and the political aggressiveness of the Atlantean race, they misused the power which they had acquired which made the trauma and the tragedy inevitable.

ATLANTEAN MAN AND HIS RETURN

Many of those who lived upon the earth during both mid Atlantis and the latter period are upon the earth once again now for an incarnation of particular importance. They would understand that it is vital now to constrain and restrict those tendencies in human nature which would pollute and damage the earth to such a degree, that the very nature of human existence and of all life in this dimension could be threatened at its very core.

There are several things which it is useful for Man to understand at this time in relation to that period, and the way in which manifestations can be seen through him and in him now. Sometimes even the mundane offers a link with that particular past to which you are all connected.

In the eyes of many young people, there is a desire to plait and to weave their hair upon their heads in such a manner that they produce a very fine woven texture to the hair. You will notice that in some communities, some of which are linked with certain African traditions there is a tendency to do this, even to the extreme, and amongst some Europeans and some individuals this particular fashion is now to be found in men as much as it is in women. This is because during the cultures of High Atlantis, which most here will have experienced, and towards its last days, one of the styles of dressing the hair was very similar to that of a tightly woven plait, small and very fine. In many cases it was worn exclusively with no free strands of hair whatever.

The reasons for this are mixed, but in one sense they represent the strands of life being woven together to produce a tapestry which is intricate and yet beautiful. This related to the original blending of the ten tribes or groups that made Atlantis. This was often found in ritualistic practices and it is a form of management of the physical body which links to a deep spiritual understanding within the self. This method of dressing the hair was in fact then taken by some of those who fled from Atlantis into the Mediterranean area, and of course this was especially the case within the cultures of Egypt, as they of that land sought to retain and unfold the wisdom of Atlantis and the stars.

These are mundane things but they are an indicative of a deep link in consciousness with that particular time and the time within which you find yourself now.

DANCE AND EARTH FORCES

There are other manifestations also which are significant. One is connected with the increasing interest in dance and in movement. It is now even acceptable in your western society, for people to be interested in gentle movements and methods of dancing and celebrating their own physical activity. Whilst of course we are aware of many aggressive and seemingly violent methods of movements which are sometimes promoted in your culture, nonetheless there is also an awakening of gentle forms of movement which are performed in groups where the collective energy of the group is used to raise the consciousness of those who are participating.

This is a practice which was developed in Atlantis. It was used especially during periods where those who were still spiritually in tune and had their origins from Lemuria very close to their consciousness, practised the dance in the fields and amongst those powers of the earth and nature to bring an enhanced sense

31

of communion between Gia, the earth goddess, and the human soul. This practice of course is being revived by many who seek to be in tune with the earth and to listen to what the earth says to them.

Now you find many who would like to walk the earth, to tread upon the earth, to attune to its energies and at the same time to sometimes work collectively, to dance upon the earth and to seek to bring energy and power through their own being into the ethers of the planet. This is a powerful connection with the old times, where earth energise and forces where better understood; it is a link with that period and some of the finest principles which were handed down from the Lemurian traditions, from those who understood the very beginnings of Man and his deepest and most beautiful origins.

You have been made aware for example of some of the mysterious patterns which are enfolding within certain of your crops and the areas of your countryside, and these are providing a deep mystery. It is not for us to reveal all to you of these things, for you will not even begin to understand much of them, but there are forces which are an awakening in the earth and at the same time a linking of the earth with higher minds and higher principles, some of which are at a different frequency to yourself and therefore you could not easily communicate or identify with them. But it is an opportunity for the earth to celebrate certain things of itself through the patterns of energy which it reveals, and whilst these energy patterns seem to occur, mainly in certain types of field where there is a sowing of a specific crop, these forces also exist where this has not occurred, and it is simply some of the energistic properties of those particles which enable these forces to become so visible.

It is an energy which expands rather in the form of a cone or vortex, an infinite shape, going on into an infinite form of expression and as this conical shape occurs, it produces many rhythms and counter rhythms. The forces of these rhythms produces sometimes in the ethers a very beautiful pattern which can then be reflected in certain flora and fauna upon the earth surface. It also exists, in some parts of the earth, in the soil itself, where the soil has been particularly susceptible to the movements of its more subtle force fields.

You may find in the years to come that more of these particular visual excitements begin to appear around you. It is for you to celebrate them, to have joy in them and where possible to visit them where you are doing no harm, and when you do this you will become responsive to the energies which are there, but they will always, to a degree, remain a mystery to your own culture now.

Remember here also that when you think of the earth, you must relate to the earth in a humble way, and understand that the earth is itself the physical expression of a greater soul and a great mind. There is no way in which Man can control the earth, can manipulate or destroy it. This is impossible for you to do. You can of course be an irritant to it, or you can be a blessing to it but in the run of time you will find that the earth will control itself beautifully and will do all that it has to do, to bring the necessary changes, so that it might flourish and grow into a new expression of itself. It is for Man either to co-operate or to be thrown from the earth until such a time comes when he is able to work in love and harmony with the home which he has been allowed to adopt for a brief spell in the whole of the cosmic experience.

MINERALS AND CRYSTALS

The Atlanteans, when you were of that race, had a deep understanding of the way that light could be projected through those minerals and crystals which were brought close to the surface of the earth, and the surge of interest in the use of minerals and crystals is also a celebration and memory of that period. It is really a revival of an old skill which many have within them and will seek to use and understand. The crystals act as agents and modulators for the energies which you can bring into play through your consciousness. This is the way in which many of you will remember how to work with crystals and rock formations but treat with care the power that you may unleash for misuse of this technology was central to the Atlantean crisis and subsequent demise.

We foresee a time when Man may work with the vibrations of very fine metals so that he can produce new energy forms for use in human affairs, energy forms which have never been used hitherto in the earth sphere. If you can understand that the way in which you make a machine at the present time from metals and now also from plastics is a very pedestrian method of using these resources. In due course there will be an opportunity for you to learn how the vibrations of these substances can be attuned to and used to produce remarkable frequencies of energy which you can then channel for your own benefit in life upon the earth. However, remember that the true fountain of Divine Force flows through you at all times, the minerals merely amplify a little that which is already within you.

ATLANTEAN HEALING

In Atlantis there was a deep interest in all kinds of healing. Whilst there was indeed an orthodoxy which had many parallels to your own, where there would have been the use of drugs and some kind of surgeries as you would have them today, albeit with different methodology, the approaches were similar. There was also a deeper wisdom that knew that if Man worked with the old ways to attune the spiritual forces at the centre of each particle of consciousness, then you could bring into manifestation remarkable healings and a transmuting of all that was undesirable and diseased.

We have told you in the past that there were creatures upon the earth who were grotesque and deformed, where Man had abused his relationship with the animal kingdom, and often these creatures were healed and treated by the most remarkable combinations of orthodoxy of the day and also the beautiful spiritual understandings which men could to attune to.

You are now entering a time where the opportunities are very similar and where you will be given the chance to blend the orthodoxy of the day and the highest vibrations within that orthodoxy with the spiritual truths which are contained within you. It is for you to spend time, whenever you can during each day of your lives, to listen and to be available for the inspiration and the intuitive gifts which can be given to you; that you might move closer in consciousness to revealing the beautiful spirit within you and thus enable all men to have a greater access to the healing which unfolds through spiritual understanding; through the forces of the spirit coursing through your being and the enlightenment which follows such profound awareness, as it grows and spreads through all humanity.

This will then enable Man to invoke methods of healing which have in the past seemed to be magical, beyond the normal human capacity."

SURGERY

6.11.90

"Most of the things which you would understand today are in fact a resurgence of that which has gone before.

As we have said, in the period of Atlantis there was a remarkable interest in minerals and in the way in which the energies of your sun, which of course are the energies of the Heart of God, could be used, amplified and verified, enabling their perfect direction to perform specific powerful functions. For example, certain energies of the sun, when filtered properly through the most powerful lenses which were built from crystal structures, were used for a type of surgery upon life forms so they might become healed or in some way eased of any physical problem which they were experiencing.

The surgery which you have today, which tends to use various implements such as knives, scalpels and so on is really rather a primitive surgery when placed beside that of the ray and the light science of Atlantis. The Atlanteans used this technology freely and knew it well.

THE GREAT CRYSTAL

There are diverse references recording the use of a Great crystal, the enormous crystal which was constructed by the Atlantean civilisation with the help of those from other planets and other worlds, so that they could collect and direct the energies of the sun for the fuelling of their own society, to generate power in the same way that you have power stations now to generate electricity.

This power would enable them to illuminate their cities, to produce all the energies which they needed to propel, lift, form and so on. Even the powering of their ships, aircraft and transport upon the earth at one stage depended upon their capacity to transform energies of the sun through crystalline structures which were specially faceted and constructed to produce the maximum use of energies.

The way in which crystals of course have become more widely used today is a small indication of a resurgence of that understanding, but we would emphasise here, it is a very small resurgence and a very small understanding of a science which was very profound and quite remarkable.

Sadly Man abused the knowledge he gained. Atlantis became increasingly corrupt. Men became over-active in their desires and very self-centred, that ultimately the Atlantean culture had to disappear. Man increasingly fell into the iniquity of worshipping the technology he discovered and not the source of life behind it.

INNER WISDOM

Those on earth today, tend to recall their Atlantean experiences, and sometimes, mistakenly, seek to re-live those times and create a New Atlantis. This is a mistake and can never be, for Man has moved forward. He now has a great opportunity to revive his contact with his Inner Wisdom and live once again in the realm of causes and not the realm of effects.

His drive towards a greater spirituality and understanding of Human Brotherhood will far outstrip the limitations of Atlantean consciousness.

The New Man unfolding, will draw upon the good in all his other experiences, and blend them into his new thinking, a new mission on Earth and an Age of Soul Awareness.

You live in exciting times.''

MEDITATION UPON THE 12 POINTS

"May the Divine Being illumine your minds. May each one of you here be blessed by one of the twelve petals of the sacred rose which brings for us the cross of denial through the unfoldment of the personal self in the Divine Essence of the soul. Here we have the twelve petals of the rose delighting upon the points of the Star of Wisdom. As you inhale the rose, the rose will present to you the power and beauty of all that is good. It will perfume your consciousness, lift your spirit and thus each of you has a petal which is precious and special for you in the light of the star of the twelve points, the Heart Star. Meditate upon this star frequently, for it is a doorway through which the truth can be expressed to you.

May the Lord of Life bless you and be with you always, lighting your hearts and may His fragrance uplift your spirits.

And so it is."

FIVE

EARTH ENERGIES

''The earth has a vast and deep consciousness fulfilling many roles . Some of you have been aware of the ethers and the soul-ethers of the earth. You are also aware of the emotional patterns which work around these ethers and beyond, tapping into the deepest feelings of the earth and at the same time blending the highest thoughts of those who live upon it.

There is also of course the understanding that within the earth, as well as upon the earth, there are many states of being. There are those beings who live within the earth, who have an existence which is very different from your own, but nonetheless, they are creatures who have a consciousness and live within the confines of the earth's structure.

Many forces, experiences and types of existence which you would consider strange and even diabolic, live within the physical form of the earth, indeed they are simply performing their role and in no sense need they cross paths with your own functions here.

At the deepest centre of the earth, the point at the core of this planet's consciousness, there is the light of a great and marvellous Being, and His inner light and eternal flame enables the earth to sustain its physical nature.

From the centre of the earth, moving to the surface of the earth, there is a continual exchange of energies, forms and dynamic patterns which ultimately manifest as the earth's surface. There is also a flow upon which those things which are returned to the earth, their more subtle energies and natures, are absorbed deep, deep into the earth where they are refined by the fire of the Being who is the earth. In time they are returned to the surface of the earth and there they vivify, give life to the very substance of the earth and its environment itself.

This exchange of power and force is perpetual. It is the

responsibility of human kind to be aware of this exchange, to work with it and to allow this continuous cycle of events to work as effectively and beautifully as it can.

It is important to understand that in your own being, at both the physical and the etheric levels, there are particles which are intelligent particles which are given to you from the consciousness of He who ensouls the earth, the great Being of whom the earth is a part or physical manifestation. He gives to you much of your consciousness and allows you to exist in part of His own Being, to enjoy some of your own growth.

ALTERING EARTH FORCES

Those subtle earth energies and patterns of which you can sometimes detect a small part when you attune to the subtleness of the earth, they are a small yet significant part of the forces of the Great Being who ensouls your planets and from your own point of view all of these patterns are good. Your relationship to them is really a question of your awareness, inner balance and the manner in which you make your attunement to the earth. There is never, for example, any need to attempt to alter a pattern of energy around the earth, for in due course the earth and the Mind which governs the earth will determine how best any change may or may not manifest.

Your role as a being upon the earth is to learn to follow your own Solar Light, soul body or inner light, the light of the spirit within you; to have such equilibrium and poise that you can assimilate the effects of all energies and be given some increase in your own vibratory rate because of such association and encounter.

We often hear words condemning some of the energies or force fields in the earth, that they are negative and that they are destructive and must be changed or redirected in some way. This is a very relative idea and in a sense it is peculiar to human consciousness at this time. As far as the earth is concerned, its energies simply are, and they each fulfil a particular function.

POLARITIES

In your own individual body you could not survive at this time without polarities. At this time you need the extremes of force to provide the maximum possibility for your own physical expression, and therefore, those polarities which you understand as positive and negative are essential. Without them you would not exist in this particular environment at all.

The same is true for the earth. The earth must have both positive and negative polarities and it must have within its physical structure pockets of both types of energy field and both types of energy line, and it is a mistake for Man to consider those forces which are difficult for him to encounter to be those which should be altered and changed. This is both arrogant and misinformed.

It is, from our point of view, dangerous for Man to even seek to tamper with the energy fields of the earth. His responsibility is to attune to those forces and to live his life according to them, to live in harmony, to live in conjunction with them.

This is the true role for Man and it is the only role which can lead to success, which can lead to a happy, purposeful, healthy existence upon the earth plane, in all its dimensions.

Those of you here who are sensitive to the earth, its lines of force and the mind of the earth, you are to be blessed. Recognise that the planet is quickening the speed of resonance and vibration in its own energy fields. Much that is dross, much that is of no real importance, is being shaken off from the earth and will be rejected. Things are changing very rapidly at your level. The negative energy lines are crucial in this cleansing — do not change them but change yourselves if necessary.

Remember that the level at which you can understand the changes, that of the intellect, is a very limited one and there are new energies, thoughts, ideals and purposes coming into and around the earth which your own conscious lower ego is not capable of understanding. The great healing is occurring in the depths of your soul and can only be known from that plane, the plane of the true self.

Be joyful for what you are taught and understand that the

earth is taking great strides forward in its evolution. You must be in tune with the earth from within your own spirit.

ENERGIES IN THE MIDDLE EAST

One thing to acknowledge about the Middle East is that in the earth itself the energies around Iraq, Turkey and Iran are of a particular volatility. That is why very often there are found to be earthquakes and disruptions in the earth's crust.

There are two points of energy of particular importance. One is in southern Turkey and one is in northern Iraq and they are both beginning to alter the frequency at which they rotate or spiral. As this occurs so there may be disturbances which could materialise into the physical earth itself. But more important than this, it will possibly also come into the consciousness of those who live in that particular area.

This is why conflict of a human kind is always likely at this time, although not inevitable, in that particular area of the earth. The inhabitants of these regions are having to deal with their own karma, with their own evolution as beings as well as with their racial and ethnic karma, and they are also having to be attuned to the karma of the earth and the evolution of the earth beneath them.

So it is a very difficult time to be an Arab and to live in that part of the world, and all the Arabic nation need your thoughts of love and peace, that they might be helped by it to grow in wisdom, knowledge and in compassion for themselves and for the whole of humanity. Then they will understand who they are, the earth and the manner in which the earth functions within the Divine Plan.

CO-OPERATION WITH THE EARTH

The earth in certain respects, is also an extension of yourself and the earth will respond to your own thoughts and feelings. At the same time you cannot govern or control the earth, the earth cannot be manipulated, it would simply work its own destiny through, either in co-operation with human kind or ultimately without that co-operation. It is up to humanity. It is up to you."

SIX

EVOLUTION

This selection of extracts considers matters relating to Man's spiritual and racial evolution, and both the influence and importance of different geographical areas of the earth.

18.9.91
"We have said to you on many occasions we are in a turn of evolution which is very powerful and formidable, and as the movement of Man's awareness moves up through to another dynamic level, so it is necessary to alter the vehicle in which consciousness can explore, gain and develop its truth.

You will know Man is an evolutionary being. It is true to say that Man was created, for in a sense the original idea which is Man was given manifestation within the mind of the Great and Powerful Being whom you refer to as God. In the Mind of this Being the idea of Man came forth and was presented into consciousness, and thus a part of the Divine, the Absolute Being, came into a glorious and beautiful expression.

This was the birth of the Man the Being as you know yourself, and he was given opportunity, part of which was the option of his descent into matter, and also his coming into the earth and experiencing the pattern of a physical life here. We would add here that in no sense was this descent compulsory or an imposed part of Man's evolution. It was an option, it was a possible path which Man could tread and thus many of the souls who were bred into this particular idea, decided to walk this earth and other 'earths' and many times have we spoken of the difficulties Man experienced as he became increasingly immersed in the physical plane and its illusion.

As time goes by, we see the pattern of Man falling further and further away from his Divine origins and moving into the concept of separation, which was perhaps at its most acute before the birth of the man Jesus, who became the Christ Mind upon the earth.''

THE NEGRO

22.2.89

''You are aware of the concept of Atlantis and the truth of that idea, for we have spoken to you on that subject before. You are also aware of other epochs and other times where there were other races of earth men, one of the most notable being that of 'Lemuria'.

Lemuria was a time where Man was Negroid or of that type of physical person. Yet the nature of his spiritual consciousness was in many ways particularly fine and when this is related to his physical development it is seen that the Man of those particular times had understanding of himself as a Cosmic entity which was subsequently lost in the overall developments of human consciousness.

The Negroes which you see today, particularly within the Continent of Africa and also upon many islands which are found to be within the Pacific, and Australia have a link with that physical form.''

THE MONGOL

''It is also true to say that when you look at the time of Atlantis, which was a particularly challenging period in the development of the human consciousness, we are dealing with a racial group which would evolve through several different physical types upon the earth, especially those remnants which you find with the more Eastern appearance and the Oriental type of body, like that of the Mongol. It is interesting to remember that it is largely through their own culture that much of your true understanding of the spirit of Man comes into being today.''

7.11.90

''In this (Atlantean) period Man became a very selfish creature, a creature who was very war-like, one who was extremely acquisitive, one who would seek to control, to impose, to manipulate. One who believed in self above all things.''

20.11.91

''The Atlantean race and its seven sub-races were potentially very beautiful but unfortunately they became less and less in tune with their higher natures and ultimately began to destroy themselves through their own wickedness and through the perversion of the talents and gifts which they had unfolded.

SEMITES AND ARYAN MAN

It became necessary for a new race to emerge and this began through those who wished to come into the earth as Semites. Eventually, from the Atlantean race (which had a sub-race called the Semites) there began to unfold a new race, a race which was very much the race which you are members of now.

This was the unfoldment of the Aryan principle in Man taking many thousands of years; this was the Aryan incarnation, and thus your own particular racial group came into focus upon the earth. The Aryan race was developed from a point in the Far East known now as the 'Gobi Desert' but at that time as 'Lake Gobi'. From here, in a place which was known as 'Shambala,' the Great White island upon Lake Gobi, the culmination of Atlantean consciousness could flow and give the seed to the New Root race of Mankind.

At the same time the unfolding of the new Aryan race could begin and this racial grouping migrated into many parts of the earth. It moved into India, into Burma, across into Persia and the Arabian Peninsula, into Africa and especially Egypt and also across into that which is now France and Germany. It also touched Greece within its own powerful culture, that the Greeks began to influence the whole of Europe and beyond.

It is interesting to note that the Greek link was essentially the one which stimulated a deep and beautiful love of music in human consciousness and through this particular and beautiful time came the Celtic connection, which is so evident in western spiritual and metaphysical cultures. So many of your myths and legends have their identity closely associated with that which is considered the 'Celtic'.

Eventually the new Aryan principle began to unfold. Unfortunately although many men upon the earth now have adopted an Aryan form, they do not in any sense have anything beyond Atlantean consciousness, for they have not developed the level of spirituality necessary to become initiated at the level of Aryan experience. And so, whilst there are many who come into Aryan bodies, there are but a few who are Aryan initiates.

AQUARIAN MAN

There are still other Aryan groups to consolidate and develop their own natures. They can be found especially in Eastern Europe amongst the Slavonic peoples. There is a flowering to come, which is the racial group of the new consciousness, the new place and the new time. This racial group will bring forth the new Aquarian race, those who would bring the Aryan wisdom unto its beautiful climax of attainment.

It is a very challenging time, a very beautiful one where we have to be prepared to relinquish the patterns of the past and adopt new vibrant patterns for the future.

But for now, the times are difficult and the way forward is for all to have thoughts of love and of peace in their hearts. It is for Man to understand the power of the collective mind. To share through the Aquarian principles, which are coming and are indeed with you now, to love and to bind to each other so that you and I and all beings may share the bounty and true affluence of life as given to us originally by our Creator, God.

CHAKRAS AND CHANGES ON EARTH

You know that within your own bodies you have areas of particular force and power, described within various traditions as 'Force Fields', as 'Chakras' or within your modern parlance they are often referred to as 'Psychic Centres'.

However you wish to refer to them, they are particular foci of force which synthesise energy fields which in turn have a powerful effect upon the area immediately adjacent to it within all human levels of consciousness, including the physical body.

This is also true of the earth. You will ascertain places of particular interest and power where the subtle influence of that point is felt considerably at some distance from it in the hinterland surrounding its centre.

There was a time when there was a special development of certain planetary power centres which are found in the east of the world, to give a special spiritual ascendancy to those regions but as you will see and understand there has been a gradual shift of influence.

There has always been considerable power and involvement in the areas of the Middle East and the provinces which you would now understand to be Iran and Iraq and also around the Holy Land, Egypt and much of the land surrounding the Mediterranean. Here there has been an important focus of Spiritual power, hence the Prophet Mohammed was revealed in this area, as was the Master Jesus before the assimilation of the Christ Spirit and many others who came to teach upon the earth.

However, it is now necessary for us to follow this focus as it develops within the European and the North American context, for we are looking now at a time when Europe in particular will become very important and the United Kingdom will have a particular spiritual significance in preparing the way for the New Consciousness.

There are legends which connect the United Kingdom with the land which we knew as 'Atlantis' and there are those who feel that the west of this country in particular was in some way or another connected to the Continent of Atlantis.

This is true, and there is, without any question, physical and geological evidence within some parts of the United Kingdom, particularly Ireland and around the North West of Scotland where the terrain has qualities similar to those found in certain areas to the North and the North East of Atlantis.

THE IRISH QUESTION

Consider also Ireland. It is very significant that it is a land of turmoil upon which there is much argument and difficulty.

In Ireland there seems to be strife, fighting and conflict of so many different kinds. This is an awakening within the hearts of men which they find difficult to understand, and because of this the energy and the power which comes to Mankind from this particular geographical location is inclined to confuse and to resurrect within the minds of those who live upon that particular plane, feelings of negativity, disdain and anger which feeds the terrible atrocities often seen in Ireland.

It is also important to recognise that you have in Ireland the descendants of those who lived upon Atlantis and who were also in a state of enmity. Those who are found within the area of Scotland, living near to the west coast and the Hebridian Islands and beyond, were in many respects connected to the thought patterns and the genetic understanding of a group of people who resented much of which had occurred within Atlantis, particularly the corruption and confusion which led to the debauchery, the warfare and to all the negative patterns within that culture.

They are still very much in tune with the thought patterns of latter Atlantis and therefore they both bring forth an old war, acting it out upon a new stage and in a new time.

In karmic terms, it is true to say that those who are in conflict in Northern Ireland in particular, are re-living by their own choice a conflict from the time of Atlantis, when there was much darkness and sorrow within that continent. They are here to learn and to re-examine that which they did before.

Sadly, we are yet to see any major progress, although we can see that there are moves afoot in the whole situation which in time may bring peace and a greater understanding."

6.11.90

"There is a choice now, a very real choice, and Man has to make that decision. It is the Atlantean Man who has come again. It is for him to make good that which he did so badly in that last period of the Civilisation.

If we were to look into your present life here and its society, you would understand for example that your present Prime Minister (Mrs M. Thatcher) was herself a very eminent Atlantean. She was one who was very gifted within the physical sciences and understood them extremely well. She was also one who during her life lost sight of the importance and value of the earth and the way in which the earth needed to be loved, cherished and considered, as Man sought to impose his own influence upon the earth becoming materialistic. She lost touch, as did so many, with the true life, the inner spiritual life.

Unfortunately, because of this very bad, difficult and inadequate relationship with the earth and life, the soul which you now understand to be Margaret Thatcher (she was a governor of an area of Atlantis) she and many others decided to return to seek to influence the earth again. It is for you to decide whether or not she is accomplishing those things which she sought to accomplish, but if her time is no longer fulfilling the needs of the greater time, that which is before the earth now, then of course she will have to make way for another who is more in tune with the needs and the requirements of the earth within your culture during this period.''

NEW RACIAL GROUP

18.9.91

''However, as the ascent of Man moves into another cycle, we are preparing for the new racial grouping.

There are two aspects to this preparation which are difficult, for one of the most important and dynamic forces to come into the new racial grouping is that of the Slavic peoples, for the new race will be born from the seeds of many races. This is why the greatest opportunity for this diversity to come into one particular place and then to be absorbed into a new consciousness is to be found in the northern part of America, that which you refer to as the United States.

The reason is essentially one of social and political evolution, for by its very nature the United States of America is able, and willing to absorb people from many, many cultures and in so

doing it provides the seed-bed upon which the new racial grouping can grow and emerge."

CHANGES IN USA

12.12.90

''There will also be changes possible within the United States of
America. This is especially important, for your country has a
degree of maturity in the spiritual sense which is useful and less
evident in the United States of America. There is an expanding
awareness there, but it is often shallow and sometimes it becomes
completely obsessed with areas of peripheral importance and
loses the central ideas and vision of truth. There is much fantasy
mistaken for truth, even by sincere, intelligent people.

Thus a need for a change in the consciousness in America, for
as the lands which were Atlantis and the lands which were
Lemuria rise and come nearer to the surface of the ocean; as the
shift in awareness comes and a subtle change occurs on the
surface of the earth, the land of America will become more
important, although the United Kingdom will be very special in
its spiritual role, like an older, more experienced brother.

In the course of this year (1990) we have begun to talk to you
of times which have past. We have begun to explain some of the
things which have occurred and the way in which they link with
that which is occurring now. We have explained the way in which
those who have incarnated in a very particular way during earlier
civilisations in Lemuria and Atlantis have come to the earth again
and have come here in great numbers to help in the unfoldment
of a greater wisdom which in an earlier time was either aban-
doned or ignored.

The opportunity is here now for Man, for you, to take this step
forward.''

THE SLAVONIC PEOPLES AND THEIR AWAKENING

18.9.91

''At this time there is to be seen the raising of those Slavonic
peoples, for those who are incarnating through the Slavonic race

are bringing one very important and fine vibration into the mixture of human consciousness.

This is why within Slavonic consciousness we are witnessing much disruption and many problems and difficulties and unfortunately, even as we speak to you now, in the country which is understood to be Yugoslavia there is a friction and difficulty as those who have a connection with the Slavonic conditions seek to assert their individual nature and to be an individual consciousness, at the same time seeking to understand their position within the whole framework of the new, beautiful evolution now unfolding in Man.

Thus, it was impossible for there to remain for much longer any containment or suppression of those people in Eastern Europe. They have an important role to play in the mixing and blending with those of other racial groups, that they might enable the grounding of the genetic pattern for the new racial group into which Human consciousness can grow.

NEW MAN AND GENETIC CHANGES

In the unfoldment of life sometimes a point is reached in development where we can say that something is, if not obsolete, at least not providing the best framework.

Man and his physical body is now going through the same kind of change. The change which Man sees in the things he makes, his material life, is a reflection of the change occurring within him for those changes are a reflection of his true self. Thus you are on the threshold of an exciting and very dynamic possibility.

On the extremity of America, that area which is known as California, there are connections with the even older civilisation of Lemuria. This influence combines with the re-awakening Atlantean consciousness, providing the thrust for a remarkable evolutionary pattern which can link Humanity with times before the (Atlantean) Fall of Man and lift him into the new and vibrant times which are before us.

We would suggest that in your minds you anticipate the idea of a new race of Man, for through your own seed and through

51

your own progeny will you find the structure into which the new mind can grow.

The New Man as he evolves will be somewhat taller in height than Man is now. He will tend to be lighter and slimmer than you are. He would carry on the whole, a less dense body weight and his mechanism will be more efficient with a metabolic form which is very different to that of this time. His genetic pattern will have changed as will the number of chromosomes within his DNA.

The New Man will evolve a glandular structure which will bring the psychic or chakric centres further into focus, enabling Man to listen and to talk with himself and his universe in a way which he has never done before. This is one reason why we find there is an increasing awareness and sensitivity in human beings, for you are preparing for this glandular change. That which you speak of as mediumship, as psychic sensitivity, as spiritual awareness, these levels of consciousness will be much more apparent in those who are being born to you now, and will be born in the near future.

It is a remarkable and powerful time and an exciting one.

One feature of the New Man which we have to appreciate is that the level of integration which is going to be necessary in him is so profound and so finely tuned that sometimes there could appear to be, in those who are the forerunners of this type, a degree of arrogance and even over-assertiveness, a confidence which goes beyond their apparent age and years of experience.

This is because there is a need for this particular power of integration, of assuredness and competence. As they unfold further you will begin to see a growth within the heart especially which will produce also a more loving and caring Man as well as a Man who is more confident, more able, more alert and more in tune with own powers, and his role in the Universe.

Many of those who are upon the earth now, who are able to show those tricks of psychic phenomena, will be surpassed by those who touch the heart and who, through their knowledge and wisdom, bring lightness into life, an awareness of divinity, a sense of awe, a knowledge of true and wonderful spiritual power. A power which manifests through a Loving Heart. These beings will need to show nothing, they will need to give nothing, they will need to demonstrate nothing. They will simply bring their love forth into life and through that love draw all men into a great, new common bond of brotherhood and enlightenment.

AUSTRALIA

We would mention perhaps some words in relation to the Continent which you understand to be Australasia. There is a significance to Australia which has a particular spiritual potency, and perhaps this could explain why the awareness of that region is growing, for it too will seek to assert itself. It too will seek to demonstrate its role as a nation and as a community, for it is shaking off its adolescence and moving towards maturity in the way that it relates to other older but in no way superior societies such as your own.

This continent has a link with Lemuria and this is especially evident along the eastern side of Australia. It is that coast which is especially energised by its connections with the light of lights and truths which relate to the past of the ancient civilisation of Lemuria. Thus you will find Australia's role, especially as the polarity of the earth begins to change, becoming increasingly significant — economically and spiritually.

THE SPIRIT OF UK

If we return briefly to consider Britain. There is a sense of spiritual freedom in the United Kingdom, in Great Britain, which few other countries have been able to enjoy to the same degree. Your community has allowed the unfolding of a special jewel here, for in the jewel of this Kingdom there is a preciousness and though it is a relatively small community, it is one which the light of the free spirit burns very brightly. Through this Kingdom which in itself has absorbed so many, many different lights and racial traditions, will the new vision be seen. Although it will not grow and emerge here as such, it is through this jewel that the new souls and the new race will be seen, understood and tempered by a unique maturity.

c

Even though that land which is the United States of America is now becoming so important, it was the spiritual freedom and energy which came through your (UK) particular community, then placed within the United States of America that has set a pure vibration for the new awareness. It could be argued that as a colonial power Britain was indeed often vindictive, often very strict and inhibiting to those over whom it had some control and dominion. Nonetheless, at the core of the British consciousness there has always been this Light of Freedom and it is this particular light which America, the United States needed, so that it might become the perfect home for the new light, the new understanding and the new souls.''

SEVEN

PERSONAL POWER AND LOVE

"During your time upon the earth you are given many, many opportunities, and all of those opportunities are there for your growth and your unfoldment as a being. It is important always to acknowledge that in the way life confronts you, you are being given a door through which you may travel into a greater awareness of yourself and to a deeper understanding of the patterns of life. Therefore, however difficult circumstances may appear before you, however challenging life may seem, you must acknowledge always that you are an aspect of God and that which is before you, you make plain so that you understand and overcome it.

You must recognise that you never encounter circumstances or challenges in your path which you have not the power and wisdom to deal with satisfactorily, for there would be no point in a life such as that.

Know always that you are the children of a God and through you that God is seeking to express His Love, and therefore it is in the Mind of God that you should be His heart. It is in the Mind of God that you should be a vehicle for the qualities of the Heart. It is the Will of God and the Plan of the Masters, that Mankind upon the earth should manifest love in all its power, in all its dignity and in the depth of its warmth and care. And so, when you take stock of your lives and begin to examine the nature of your own reactions and responses, you should always do so in the light of that understanding.

You must ask yourself the questions which say of you, "How much and how deeply did I share the Love of God which is within me? How much did I show the compassion and the forgiveness which is mine to give? How much did I enrich this life by my being here? How is life blessed by me?"

CHANGES

These are the questions you should ask of yourself each and every day. You will notice and you will understand that you are in a phase of your life where you will see much change. We have spoken many times of the changes in the earth and the way in which the current social nature of your life and the economic and political pictures will now have to change considerably.

It is not as if God in some mysterious way is seeking to play a game with his children and throw them into confusion and disarray. It is within the pattern of things that Man should become more aware of his interdependence with all life, both human life and life in other dimensions and kingdoms here on the earth, and in this surge forward, which we must make to gain new ground in our understanding, it is inevitable that much of the past, however well it has served, will be moved away as we move into a new consciousness.''

GOD IN YOU

''It is a time for great courage, a time for each one of you here to be unafraid and to be assured that the Light of the Father IS IN YOU IN ITS ENTIRETY. There is nothing which is beyond your comprehension and expression. And thus, however life appears to be, if you can be at one with your own spiritual core and know that God is not with you but IN you, then you have nothing to fear.

Those alterations which must occur around you will be merely the clearing of the mist before a clear vision comes into play, and just now, if you look back and see a view of life as it was some twenty, thirty or forty years ago and compare it with the status which you have now, you must consider that those things which were once of use and once a reflection of Man's awareness, can no longer be satisfactory.

This is the case now for so many things.

TRANSITIONS

You have amongst you now on the earth many wonderful beings who have come into incarnation so that they might be of service in the transitions which occur. Many of you will be stirred into a new direction, perhaps something which was with you for a long time suddenly is taken from you. It may be that your occupation is taken from you. It could be that one you have loved suddenly decides that they have completed their part of this pattern and move away from this earth, leaving you behind! It may be that you have reached a point in your life where you can see and you know in your heart that some change is inevitable for you.

When this occurs it is the spirit in your own heart tapping on the door of your consciousness and saying to you, "You must now be ready to work for life and to honour those things which you know are for the good of yourself and for all men. It is time for you to follow the path of truth and to serve in whichever practical fashion you can, in tune with the highest principles of life."

When you have such an opportunity you should see it as such, for that is what it is.

If in your heart now there are feelings of unsettledness, a desire to change, then that is the spirit of your heart whispering to you, "Now is the time, it is the time for you to look at who you are and what you are doing." Others around you may question some of the judgements you make, some of the choices you decide to follow, but if you truly wish to serve Mankind and at the same time enrich your spiritual fire, there will be, we can promise you, no greater joy and no greater prosperity or success than that which is the following of your truth."

TWELVE POINTED STAR

"You are spreading the light and the truth of Divine conscious-ness to all men and when this light is offered to you, we suggest that you focus upon the image of the Twelve-pointed Star. The Twelve-pointed Star is significant in that it produces a vibration in your own etheric world which enables forces to flow between the highest spiritual level of consciousness to travel through the minds of the Masters into the Astral and then into the ethers which are a part of your world. This links the Hearts of all beings.

It is because the power behind the Twelve-pointed Star is so magnificent and complete that it is a key which is unlocking windows, windows which in themselves are the channels through which the light can come.

It is now important for you always to be conscious of this particular link and to recognise that when you focus upon this wonderful symbol, it will channel through your own being the most magnificent light. Your role as a being is to not engage in directing that light in a specific manner but to allow the Melchizedek to use His own mathematical ingenuity to provide the frequencies of light which will best be used in the affairs of men.

Your channel should be open and pure. You should allow the forces to come freely through your mental and emotional selves into your etheric realms. As this occurs you will find and discover that the influence for good and for peace will grow to bring remarkable changes in your world.

Your role is to be attuned, to open your heart to the Twelve-pointed Star and the light which it is radiating to you, and as this occurs, you then open your heart to humanity and to the world on which humanity is found incarnate. You are then doing your work, you are providing your light, your force through which good can then be brought into more profound manifestation.''

CHANNELS OF LIGHT

"We would ask you at this time to be conscious of your world, to understand that whilst in your own minds here, there is a growing sense of peace because you are all upon the path of self-understanding, you are all seeking to give, to love and to promote that which is beautiful, that which is kind, that which is the true smile of God, yet, in your world as a whole there are still many human souls who are living in utter darkness.

Their roots go down into the bowels of the earth, they are

touched by the dimmed lights of Hades and thus they bring pain into the earth. They have a perverse pleasure in the twisted mechanisms of their mind which would seek to bring joy through pain, and thus their laughter is the laughter of humiliation, their fulfilment is the suppression of the flowering of human kind through killing and through inflicting all kinds of indignity.

As we look upon the surface of your world we ask you to understand that when you come together as you have done on this night, you bring into the ethers of the earth fresh and more powerful light. You give a framework upon which the angels can build Temples of Light and Peace. This Light which can then be channelled around the Earth to bring into all Men's hearts some peace, some opportunity to rise from the darkness and its illusion, into the umbrella of light and love.

There are souls who are passing into the Astral light, as we speak, who are doing so at the hands of torturers. There are souls passing into the Astral light as we speak who are doing so through the bullet of a gun and through the blade of a knife, inflicted with hatred and with the venom which would not even befit a serpent. Your light here can help them as they move into the Astral consciousness, often disorientated, often in shock, often in pain and in sorrow, sometimes not even aware that they have passed from one life into another.

And your light will bring rescue. It will bring to them the opportunity to focus upon their new reality and then make their progress in the Astral life of self-understanding before they move higher and higher to touch their mental principle and reach out for their soul.

You are engaged in this work at all times, whether you would know so or not, and at this time you, in this particular group, have assisted us to bring the transition of at least seventeen souls who were trapped very close to the earth. In two particular instances they were soldiers who had passed into the Astral light during the conflict in the Gulf area and who were of English nationality. They have now been turned into the light, they have met those who went before them from their own families and they are at peace. And for that we say thank you.''

EIGHT

EXTRA-TERRESTRIAL CONTACT

"We have spoken to you of those who come to the earth from exalted levels of being and also mentioned that there are beings communicating with the earth from other planets and also from beyond this solar system, from other parts of your galaxy.

There are always on your earth those who come from other parts of the solar system and the galaxy, but they exist usually no closer than the ethers and very often exist even at a finer level of mind than that, a subtle overtone of the physical plane. Often, as you walk or travel in a particular place or direction upon the earth, you will feel that you have others with you, close to you. Sometimes these are extra-terrestrial beings who have come close to the earth to engage with you, to be with humanity, to observe, to teach, to share and just occasionally also to learn from the activities upon this planet.

However, there are one or two other things important to consider here.

At the higher levels of human government and within the senior positions in the military establishments of the most developed and advanced nations upon the earth there has been communication of a very profound nature with beings from other worlds, and we would say to you that at several positions or places upon the earth there are physical manifestations which are the residues of extra-terrestrial visitation.

There are, in the United States of America, at least three manifestations of physical craft which the authorities there have within their control. They may have been unable to substantiate where they come from, and they also have been unable to understand the molecular structure of the substances from which these craft have been made.

There are those who have learned certain technological and astronomical and even biological ideas and principles from

60

extra-terrestrial minds which have been able to link with the minds of Man, to inspire and to teach them.

Remember of course, that Man himself does not come from the earth in a true sense. It is only the present physical form which has been nurtured upon the earth, but the essence of Man is from beyond this planet. The channel who is speaking to you here or through whom we are communicating, is himself an entity from beyond this solar system and he has little connection with this solar system other than some three incarnations upon the earth.

This is true for many beings.

There are entities who have come into physical manifestation but are of extra-terrestrial origin, walking the earth now. Some of them live as if they were ordinary human beings within the culture of your earth, for there are some entities who have managed to produce a physical manifestation which is almost identical to the main streams of the human root races which have been on the earth thus far. They live and walk amongst you now.

So you can see that there are others upon the earth with whom you could communicate about their immediate extra-terrestrial origins and it would be possible for you to gain access to their parts of the galaxy, not simply through travel *per se*, but more because of your ability to link in mind with their experience and for them to convey to you and through you the truth of their own origins.

COMMUNICATION

Should you wish to communicate with those who are not from the earth, it is possible to do so. We come through the channel here in this particular manner, and in a sense you could even consider us to be extra-terrestrial, for in certain respects we are, but our consciousness is working within the mental planes of this solar system for the most part. The Melchizedek comes from beyond this solar system, and the Christ has indeed the seeds of His evolution from beyond your own galaxy, but if we bring all these things together and try to understand their particular purpose, perhaps we must realise most of all that at any moment you can

D

be in tune with visitors from other worlds and from other planets and they can come to you should you wish to be in touch with them.

Always if you seek communication, do so from a focus of love. Seek to be in tune with those who come to you through the light of the Christ, the Compassionate One, the Cosmic Light of Love.

Also seek to link with a view, not to sensationalise, or for quick personal gain or influence, but for spiritual wisdom and knowledge, that you might become more aware of your True Self and thus a greater servant for Humanity and Creation.

If you ask to be unified with these entities, then in some way or another they will come to you and give evidence of their own origins and their wisdom.

Very often, in the course of your daily lives, you may find that you spend time with others who know consciously that they are from another planet, from another part of this great and wonderful Universe, but they will link with you as and when they choose, and they will communicate with you only when you are ready to be at one with them and to be in tune with their great ideas and principles.

Remember, however, that the greatest communion is that of a Man with his own soul."

NINE

EVERYTHING HAS MEANING

"Every time you are involved in activity, you feed back to the heart and to the soul light in the chambers of your heart the experience and understanding which you gain for each and every moment of your life.

This is particularly significant. It means that for every possible second of time in your existence upon the earth, there is nothing which is insignificant or without meaning. There is nothing that you do in the course of your day which is not of the greatest significance.

Because of who you are upon the earth plane, because of the way in which your consciousness has been structured and limited by years and years of restricted thought patterns and lack of appreciation of the inner self, you tend not to understand the value and indeed the importance of all things which you encounter. The dusting of your home, the sweeping of your floor, the removal of those things which have no further purpose and discarding them in waste disposal bins in your home, those moments which seem unimportant, are of immense significance. For the removal of those things which seem to have no further place in your life is of itself an act of recognition of the cycles of life and the manner in which we can move from one set of experiences to another. For the carton which once contained an item of great importance is being given to you, albeit very briefly, and in due course it is returned to life, to the earth, back into the energy field from whence it came.

The peeling of the vegetables for your table, they too have a purpose in bringing goodness and vitality into your life by means of those things which you can eat and from which you can extract nutrients, nutrients which will give you power and energy to exist in the physical realm. Even those peelings which you have taken from them which are no longer of any practical use to you, are your offering back to the earth. They are for you a link with the cycle which brings all things to fruition and then releases them so that they may travel backwards, upwards, forwards or sideways into another experience. Thus the pattern of growth, change and alteration of state and purpose continues.

If we were to consider for a moment here the peelings of a vegetable such as the potato, which is one which you would eat. They would seem to be very insignificant and of no consequence to you. Yet, as you peel away the skin of this vegetable you take for yourself that which you are able to identify as for your good, which you can absorb and be fuelled and energized by, and then those parts which are of no further use you will discard. You may place them perhaps upon your garden or in the refuse bins, but ultimately you are returning back to life and to its cycles those things which you have been allowed to use very briefly for the convenience of your existence in this physical world.

Your whole life should be a contemplation of truth and experience and each moment of your life should be given special value, should be given a consideration which shows you are grateful for each moment, not only those moments which are of obvious material significance but also those moments such as the sweeping of the floor and dusting of a room.

We can assure you that in Cosmic terms the way in which you deal with the dust in your home is as important and significant as the manner in which you deal with experiences of fame and fortune and those times which would seem to be of great acclaim.

In terms of the soul and the manner in which the soul responds, those simple experiences are often those which etch the most beautiful patterns and light upon the body of the soul. And those things for which we would feel we might gain the most wonderful accolades, are frequently of much less significance than the minute day to day experiences.

That is why that which is referred to as spiritual growth is often more powerfully experienced in the apparently mundane aspects of life than in those moments of apparent grandeur.

During this time there is a need for a sharp increase in the way in which we work to project the thoughts of love and understanding in the earth. As we are seated here in this room there are souls leaving the physical life, moving into the higher, subtle realms of consciousness. Some are moving through mental processes which are just as natural but nonetheless encased in trauma and in shock, and, of course, because of the nature of war, there are those, as we speak to you, who are passing from the physical life into the consciousness of the lower Astral planes, and they will need help and guidance in many cases, for the passing for some will be quick.

Recognise that a group such as this helps those who work from the higher planes with the Masters and the Brotherhoods to focus upon the earth energies of light, peace and understanding which act as ladders of consciousness for those who are leaving the earth plane, especially in shock or in trauma.

You provide a beautiful power which draws the souls of those who are bewildered and lost, that they might then find their path to the light of the next reality which bids them and waits for them to arrive. Know that during this hour we have spent with you this night, your power and love will have been of great value to us.''

TEN

ASTRAL PLANE CHANGES

This communication was given to a small group in November 1992. It considers changes on the Astral or Emotional plane and the effects it might have upon us all.

COMMUNICATIONS FROM HIGHER LEVELS

10.11.92

''One of the essential functions of the contact which we endeavour to make is to establish some understanding of the principles which are at the root of the changes in human consciousness and the manner in which we can best co-operate with the instincts and the finer knowledge of your higher self, as it seeks to beckon the rest of you into a new and more vibrant phase of human existence.

There are of course at this time many communications with the earth which are given to human souls through channels such as this, and we would say to you this first and foremost that in your evaluation of any words or ideas which are placed before you, you must always work from the position of your own knowledge and your own inner wisdom. For it is through your own mind and heart that you will gain the new insights and if any particular approach is seriously discordant with the highest principles in your own consciousness, then it is of course your responsibility to reject or place to one side those ideas if they do not resonate in the chambers of your own heart and its goodness.

You must remain loyal to the joyful spring of your own being. Never abandon that voice within your being which is loyal to you and ever exalts you to a higher appreciation of life and a higher appreciation of your own role in the pattern which is before you.

We believe that at this time there are attempts from the darker sides of consciousness to place Man in some further degree of thraldom whereby he exchanges one illusion for another, and it is imperative therefore that you recognise that it is only in the offering of truth which is both liberating and is a further celebrating of your glory and your love which can be of any substance. Where a teaching or an idea places you at the feet of a master whereby you are a slave to his prompting and demands, then we would suggest that such urgings and such prognostications and teachings are of questionable nature and should be treated as such.

Always assume a position as a being of light and vast potentials, who is being spurred and inspired into further action rather than being goaded or bullied or even placed in a fearsome position whereby your willingness does not emanate from a point of joy but rather from a point of duty or even fear.

EMOTIONAL CHALLENGES

We consider that for human kind the greatest difficulty is the transcending of the emotional self, for so much of your consciousness and of your awareness is placed within the emotional structures which humanity has placed around itself. The greater task at this time is the transmuting of this field of force into a lighter and clearer realm through which your consciousness may travel, that you may claim the higher ground in true awareness and become the Sons of Light which you once were truly intended to be.

At this particular moment in your history we understand that there is a vast reservoir of consciousness which is being cleared from the perimeters of your planet and therefore from the human experience. From your point of view it is as if the cloudy and muddy waters of the consciousness are being filtered and cleared to a crystalline sparkling form that you may more easily see through the darkness and into the light. This is now happening within the light of the emotional and desire worlds, that which is often referred to as the Astral light or the Astral world.

So much of human reaction is a rebounding of thought upon this vast conditioning Astral sphere and as humanity plays out its role upon the earth especially, there is an interchange with the dynamics of this plane which Man has created for himself. The interaction with this vast and very dense field produces an illusion which confines most of humanity in a framework which is a cyclic, inhibiting and destructive pattern as it obscures the understanding, the true understanding, of the solar-self, of the light-self and of the spiritual force which is at the core of all human function but of course is obscured by this density and the apparatus which it uses to perpetuate its own illusion. From the illusion grows further processes which are of themselves yet more illusion and more fantasy.

At this moment there is an attempt which will unfold into a successful conclusion whereby the vibrations of this plane are being cleared and opened into a new and purer form.

EFFECTS ON RELATIONSHIPS

This has an powerful effect upon your individuality and the very essence of your nature. Perhaps if we look at the more difficult aspect of this experience we can understand that within the emotional and desire nature of the individual, there is a tendency for possession and limitation, and many of the relationships which have been formed by humanity in its journeying over the last epoch have been based upon the Astral or emotional self.

Therefore, as the cleansing and the clearing begins to take effect, those of you who are within the vanguard of this experience will find many of the emotional trappings of your life peeling away, clearing your path and your own vision, and thus the dynamics of your relationships with each other will become clearer, more sharply focused. As this unfolds so the exchange which ensues will clear away many illusions and where a relationship is not founded upon the energies of the heart and of the qualities of true soul experience, then of course it may begin to prove a relationship under strain and in difficulty.

Where the relationship is formed through the heart and the dynamics of the soul are in place for an exchange which brings of itself a special participation in the unfoldment of the greater plan, then those relationships will be even more secured within their exchange and they will take on a fresh and more vibrant dimension of experience, greater than ever before in the human period of history.

You may discover in your own life that the nature of your relationships with those who are close to you will change and will explore new avenues and new dimensions. Thus there is a quicker exchange of relationships, with some dissipating and disappearing and others appearing and growing, and the central relationships which are focused upon the heart become stronger, more resolute and more expansive in the manner in which they radiate into life the essence of the Divine as it works its mystery through the twin dynamics of a duality.

As we move closer to the vision of the soul thus we move closer to the freedom which such a vision will bring, and the emotional constrictions which have impeded true and open relationships will begin to dissolve. Relationships will be more wonderfully expressed in the years to come.

HONESTY

You will notice that one of the features of the emotional light is the propensity to a life of insincerity, a life in which the truth is seldom shared and where deceitfulness and the obscuring of the true identity of an experience, a thought or of a feeling is often deemed to be a strength and a feature of cleverness, an expediency in life which is either desirable or at least acceptable. In the clearing which is now ensuing this will no longer be the case, for we move into a consciousness where the openness of the heart will no longer permit the illusions of deception. We move to an openness and an honesty both with ourselves and with each other. No longer will we be allowed to hide in a mask behind which we place the innermost fears of our being and behind which we hide from the truth of each other.

At this time a greater honesty is demanded of all human beings. We must not confuse honesty with aggression, with assertiveness, with a desire to impress others with our straightforwardness. It is rather a question of being open with a heart which shares the purity of its essence and the true vibration of the singular quality which it brings into this life experience.

The cleansing, this purification will also at times appear to bring to the surface conditions and feelings which many will have thought are conditions of the past. This is because of the nature of our old attitude and the tendency within the deceitfulness to submerge those things which are undesirable, into the depth of the unspoken part of our consciousness. The new reality and the clearing of the emotional self will no longer permit this act of suppression. Such patterns of thinking are now being removed. As the removal becomes more evident and more rapid, thus to the surface in our individual consciousness come many of the old patterns and forces of our emotional self which we have to recognise and then transmute into a higher force within our minds and our souls.

This is occurring within individual patterns and also within groups, sects and nations and within the community of Man itself. This is one reason why so many patterns which we thought were of the past, where strong emotions and feelings underpinned the very nature of such expressions, are beginning to surface again, but we must not in any way seek to repress them again. They must be released and transmuted through the love of our hearts, for the times now support and encourage such endeavours.

The age of conflict is passed. The age of unity is with us. If we affirm in our consciousness our unity with each other, the collectiveness of life and the inner purposes of the soul, thus we are given the power through being to turn, transmute and raise all the forces in us which are destructive, into energies of purity and light.

RE-AWAKENING TO A GREATER PAST

It is a time of opportunity and redemption of the emotional Man and his formulation into a new, more clear and outward looking creature.

It is also perhaps a wonderful opportunity for all souls to understand the awakenings within themselves, for as the emotional substance is cleared, so within your being the memories of a greater past will be resurrected in your consciousness. The memories of an inner identity which transcends the current perception of a limited and finite Man will become gradually clearer in your minds.

This awakening will come in all souls. The degree to which it will occur and the manner of its manifestation will be different according to the different natures of each one of you, but occur it will. It will affect your minds, it will affect your bodies and it will bring sharply into your thoughts the light and the purity of the spirit. Know that those who are here to assist in this elevation of consciousness, in this bringing of a new and perfect feeling, these souls are to be found in and amongst you at all times. Remember it is not always he who claims to be a master who has the light of the soul burning brightly throughout his endeavours. Many will be surprised when the realisation of who some of these great spiritual souls are, finally becomes apparent to them; for it is not always those who profess such wisdom and who claim such accolades who are the ones who possess such light.

It is often within the humility and the quietness of an open heart and soul that we find the workings of the higher levels and the true potentials to be a catalyst in the transformation of those with whom they come into contact. It is for you within your own activity to regard all souls as the potential source of the transmutation of your own light and it is in the identifying of these souls that you will provide for yourself a fresh impetus in your searching and journeying into this vast and wonderful experience.

On a practical level, considering your lives and the nature of your society, it is obvious to any soul who is alive and who is thinking clearly of the circumstances of life, that the social/economic changes which are being encountered at this time are a reflection of this purification, for you cannot open the hearts of men to an honest and pure light and yet have a reflection around that light which is not in harmony with it. It is inevitable that the structures which will not change and grow with the flow of the times must be replaced. The experience in your culture now is a remarkable opportunity for the bringing of an honesty and openness into all the affairs of men, especially those which appertain to finance and to the nature of the exchange of wealth and material energy in your cultures. For no longer can Man be motivated by greed and self-centredness and the capacity to gain over others at the material level since, in so doing, he is investing in the outer world a quality which it does not possess and he is ignoring the capacity of the true kingdom in his heart to determine the nature of his reality.

In your everyday lives, it is your responsibility to give time to those in your racial groupings who are in need when it is apparent that they are experiencing emotional turmoil. It is beholden to all men to recognise that if there is any truth in the meaning of wholeness, then it encapsulates all life and all beings. There is no space for a self-centred consciousness in the consciousness of the soul and in the proposition of an honest and emotionally liberated society. It will demand of all men a willingness to share with those who are burdened by the challenges of the time, and the consequences, even of their own karmic patterns and the manner in which the difficulties are manifesting around them. It is a responsibility for all men to be prepared to work with those who do not seem to be as fortunate as themselves, to share and to exchange, not of course to the exclusion of a degree of self-awareness and self-preservation, but at the same time you can only preserve the true quality of yourself by the manner in which you radiate the qualities of your good self. It is through your supporting of others that the new and wonderful work of redemption can be placed before you and within you.

There is a great task in place here and all men must be involved in the raising of consciousness. We have seen many times suggestions that there will be a limitation to the numbers of souls within this chain of experience who can ascend into a new awareness. This is fiction as far as we can understand, for the nature of human bonding would suggest that every soul within your chain of consciousness must and will make a transition into a higher awareness, even if this, in some respects will imply movements within movements and wheels within wheels and levels of awareness within a greater change, but it is upon each of you to be a vehicle for the transmuting of human emotional forces and the placing of all conditions within the sphere of the heart.

There are many complexities which are placed around humanity. They seem so often to be vehicles of opposition to the very truth which we seek to understand and share with you. There seem to be those who still resist the obvious flow and awakening within the hearts of so many, but like a massive wave which rolls across the ocean, there can and will be ultimately a complete movement that all must be touched by, and therefore the old must be cleared away. There is no possibility that this cannot occur. It is too important within the framework of the earth itself, of the solar system and indeed the whole of the universe in which you find yourselves at this time. There is too much in terms of development and change which has already occurred for this not to be so.

ILLUMINATION

It is perhaps important to appreciate that many souls have become trapped within the cycle of the emotional self and even between the periods of their incarnations upon this earth. In this plane of reaction, they find themselves encased in the illusion of the next life and their conception of their heaven world is merely a place in which they work through desires and still experience frustrations and thus are bonded to come back into the earth and to once again work through an illusory pattern, for they refuse to look beyond into the higher light, the higher consciousness and to see their Solar Angel beckoning them to a greater vision, a greater understanding and a wonderful position of effectiveness.

These souls especially in your earth now, who are incarnating, would not perhaps even begin to understand the words we are sharing here, but if in your consciousness you can begin to expand these ideas further, to demonstrate them in the purity of your life here, now, to use the fundamental teachings and principles which have been given through the great avatars and beings who have walked the earth, and especially through the Consciousness of the Christ, then ultimately the truth which is great and beautiful in your own being must become the truth for all men. The light which is special within your own heart will become the light which is special for all men. You, through the

Divinity in your hearts, offer the illumination to another, and this dynamic, illustrated and expressed in the mode of your life, is essential.

TRANSMUTING EXPERIENCES

There has been a tendency for those who have glimpsed some of the new vision and who have been touched by the minds from other levels of consciousness, such as we, who seek to share, to encourage, to inspire where we can, there is also a tendency to treat this reality as a disposable failure and one from which they should run as quickly as possible leaving behind the patterns of their life as if they have no responsibility for them. This you cannot do. You have a responsibility for that which you have built, and you must, through your material life and the opportunity which is given to you now, draw through your consciousness the total of your experiences of the past. As you draw that experience through your consciousness you can transmute and lighten every molecule of substance which you have encountered and create the new reality in harmony with the Angelic beings, the forces of the Spiritual Masters, and the Loving Christ in your Heart.

Thus you transmute the total experience of humanity in this round, including the darkness, the illusion, the deception, the manipulation which must be worked through and expiated. It is not within the interests of humanity for those souls who become feckless to seek to dispose of the responsibilities which they have failed to discharge.

Use your time now to live through the highest principles in your life, to absorb the love of the Christ and the wisdom that you may employ that love effectively and in a manner which is for your highest good and the highest good of your brothers and your sisters. Open the gateway to a greater reality for all men, not just for yourself. That is the secret of spiritual mastership, for it is only through service that you can unfold the greatness which is already within you and resurrect that wonderful consciousness which for so long has been submerged.

SPIRITUAL COMMUNICATION

Where there is a dependence upon the psychic nature and there is no support from a spiritual perspective, then you may find that such souls begin to encounter difficulty in the manner in which they function and much of the quality which they attribute to themselves will disappear. It is only those who are prepared to look beyond the confines of that Astral light, who will be able to recognise the new consciousness and special Divinity with which they must live and work.

Much of the spiritual communication of early times was a communication from an Astral, emotional consciousness and as the weeks and months move by, this connection will become increasingly difficult to sustain. For the souls who are focused at the Astral levels are being given help and assistance to raise their own awareness and to be involved in their own re-birth, their own re-awakening, and thus many of the qualities of that which you understand as mediumship will change and many have already experienced such differences within these functions.

The manner in which we communicate here is essentially mental and therefore it is a facility which we can continue to use so long as it is viewed to be within the highest good of those with whom we come into contact. But for all of you the pathway to your own mastership is being placed more clearly into your own hands. It requires no more than an openness of heart and a willingness to adopt the principles of loving wisdom in your affairs. If you work and live thus, you will produce a resonance within you which will transcend any difficulty and any change which you may encounter. That is all you need to do.

It is a simple task in itself, but the demands can appear rigorous for it does not require a technique, it requires an openness of being which is essential for you all in the coming times.

God be with you.''

ELEVEN

ANSWERS TO SOME QUESTIONS

Q— *'Do you think life here has a pattern, do you believe certain events with us are bound to happen?'*

"Life has a pattern for each upon the earth. No two incarnated souls upon the planet earth have been given the same objectives, and for each one of you the path you have to follow is different.

This is why when you compare your own particular circumstances with those of another, the exercise will be fruitless. For your path is for you and upon incarnation you are fulfilling prenatal commitments which you have made with guidance from others, that you might work best to achieve both the refinement of your own soul and also be a support for the endeavours of those with whom and around whom you have incarnated.

And there is an optimum pattern for life with which you come to the earth and this pattern has quite specific objectives to its operation. There are certain parameters of expression in your life, and if you depart from them, then you will discover that your life can become more difficult and more painful. But if you work within the structure which you have been given, and if you seek always, as we have already said, to understand the highest principles of life, looking for the opportunities, seeking to be full of optimism in the way that you approach your life, then those circumstances which are difficult will begin to dissolve as you progress, growing in strength and in wisdom.

Your optimum pattern will become clear to you. You will see within yourself those abilities and talents which are specific and useful, those aspects of expression which fill you with joy and good feeling, and there will be those other areas of life which for you seem to be inappropriate and not so fulfilling.

Thus there is a pattern, there is no God who plays a random

game and throws you upon the earth as if you were dice. There is a scheme to all things.

Within the pattern which you have, there are always major objectives which you, as an individual, linking with the wisdom of your soul, would seek to encounter, and these will come in the form of those you meet as fellow human beings and in the circumstances which you encounter, for you have chosen the nature of your experience.

The conflict which we encounter comes because the soul and the personality are often in conflict. The personality, that which you would understand to be the lower self, often loses its connection with its soul light and thus will go off-track and lose direction. Sometimes the battle between the soul and the personality will dominate a whole incarnation and a life will be one of conflict and difficulty with little joy, little happiness and very little true success.

But when you listen to your heart and to your soul, when you observe the nature of your patterns and see where life is calling you to go, then you will meet the objectives you have set before yourself as the next and most important aspect of your experience.

There are major objectives which we must encounter, and if we seek to avoid them then they will come before us again and again and again until we have grown sufficiently in consciousness to recognise that this is something we must overcome.

Many are ways of learning a lesson or gaining an experience, and sometimes, when we avoid a particular circumstance, it seems to disguise itself and come around again in a rather different form. It will have contained within it the necessary pattern for us to go through that we might bring into our hearts the most appropriate refinement of our soul.

Remember, you have the power to create a reality, to create a path or way of your choosing. But your ingrained belief system would currently tend to constrain that freedom. In linking with your soul, you perceive your optimum pattern, the best way forward from where you are. You know your obligations and desire to fulfil them.

This is the nature of things as we understand them. You are

given choices always, you are given freedom, but you have made many choices before you came into the earth and thus you have been involved in the setting of your pattern. If you fail to walk the path you have chosen, you would be avoiding that which you have already determined you should do.''

Q— *'On earth we have physical sense to recognise our physical fellow beings. How in the etheric do you identify each other?'*

''Remember that the ethers is much a plane or dimension of sound. Each one of you here, if you sought to develop the ability, could learn to hear the sound of the energy of another, for the ethers is the energy pattern containing the forces of the individual, and it is possible to listen and hear the vibration of the energy field of any individual.

It is also possible to listen to the ethers and to understand the sounds which all can hear. Your audiometry, your ability to hear in physical terms, is really a very small range of hearing and your ears in the physical world have a limited capacity to hear vibrations of the ethers.

You would understand, for example, that animals have a much greater range of audiometric facility than you have and they can hear the subtle sounds that you cannot. They hear etheric patterns which you and I would never perceive as human beings, and thus it is that in etheric states you would recognise another by the vibration and the sound of his etheric self. There is a form of etheric or energy vision, but it is closely linked to the Astral field.

But we would like to make one point clear here. You must recognise that the etheric level of being is very much a part of the physical world and that when you have passed from the physical life, then in due course not only do you leave your physical body to give its particles back to the physical plane of the earth, but you also eventually relinquish your etheric self too, as you make the focus of your consciousness in the Astral plane for a time.

And how do you recognise each other in the Astral world?

You recognise each other in the Astral world by the light which you show, by the quality of that light. It is easier to be seen and to see in the Astral realm than it is upon the earth. In the

Astral realm one can have the ability to see all other entities which exist within the sub-planes of the Astral plane and also be in tune with the vibrations with those who are still upon the earth.

So to summarise, we recognise each other in the ethers by the sound we produce. Each one of you is a symphony, is that not a beautiful idea? And each of you is also a creature of magnificent light, a kaleidoscope, and that is how you would recognise each other upon the Astral plane.

When you go through the death of the Astral self, which you do, and move into a higher consciousness on the lower mental planes, then you will recognise each other by your minds and the quality and dynamics of the thoughts which you experience.''

Q — *'Are you, at your level of development, aware of human spirits from planes other than earth?'*

''The simple answer to that question is yes. You will of course appreciate that the earth is one of many planes of consciousness. There are souls, and by souls we are here talking of particles of the Divine, which come not only to the earth, but can exist between incarnations, in other levels of planetary consciousness. For each of the planets of your solar system has the capacity to sustain life, but life of a quality which is extremely remote from that which you have upon the earth here.

Also understand that there are also souls whose incarnations have occurred in other solar systems and that, where these souls are sufficiently evolved, they are able to come close to the earth and to view and assist in the evolution of this solar system and its growth.

We can perhaps illustrate this point thus.

The Christ, who you would understand to be the Light which came into the Master Jesus when He was baptised in the River Jordan, the Christ had His evolution not in this solar system but in a solar system in another part of the Galaxy. When the Christ came close to this solar system, He could only express Himself through the Heart of God and thus the main focus for the Christ was through that which you understand to be your sun.

The initiation of the Christ, which all souls will go through, took place in another solar system. It is easy for us to be aware of souls whose pattern and cycle has either taken place beyond this solar system and also those souls who live upon the earth but whose development and evolution enables them to also have expressive experience upon other planets.

Man, especially modern, contemporary Man, has long basked in the illusion that he is alone in this solar system, that there is only life upon the earth and that there could conceivably be life in other parts of this galaxy and other galaxies, but it is very unlikely that that life could be sophisticated enough to come to the earth. But how wrong Man is.

There are many souls who come to the earth, to visit your planet and to move in the ethers of your planet most of the time to ensure that the growth of the earth and those souls who are upon it, are in tune with the plan for this part of the galaxy. Life upon earth is monitored, and you receive some protection, that you might not obliterate yourselves and your earth, for that could never be. It is possible, upon occasion, for those who come from other planets and other solar systems to come onto your earth and even to express themselves in physical form, and to do this they would evolve vehicles or craft which you could accept and understand, for you still perceive that travel can only be undertaken when you travel within the confines of a vehicle.

But those who have evolved beyond this level will construct an aura of protection which would translate to you to be a vehicle or a craft, but they travel because of their knowledge of the powers of light and of the fusion and exchange of light, and they come close to you often. There are also craft which exist at a more subtle physical frequency, another dimension, and you would not see them.''

TRANCE STATES AND TRANCE HEALING

Q — *'Can you speak to us about the nature of Trance Healing.'*

''Trance Healing. If we can explain the condition which we have here first.

The entity which you know and understand as He who is 'Paul', during this time with you we are able to come into his mind matter, into the 'chitta' of his own being, and through our own light share and influence his own identity sufficiently that he can become a vehicle or a channel for the thoughts and understanding which we are bringing into his mental body.

As this occurs, and to help him, we bring his own focus of awareness into a deeper dimension of himself so that he might be free from any interference in the transmission of words and ideas which we bring. This can only be done with his co-operation, with his consent, within the laws of the Universe and with the support of the angelic beings who sustain the Light of Life within him and within our own minds.

This is a process of great sanctity. It is one which should be respected and it is therefore possible for him to bring into the earth our thoughts, our love, our energies.

It is possible in certain cases for an individual to be influenced in this way, and thus a particular entity may gain control, sometimes for good and sometimes for reasons perhaps which are slightly more questionable, and as this control takes effect, the entity may wish to fulfil an obligation in his own karma or to change the energy within his own karmic pattern.

If it is an Astral entity, one whose mentality is still focused upon the Astral planes, it is perfectly possible that he would seek to work in a field which was in tune with his earth life or one of his earth incarnations, and therefore he may seek to heal in some fashion. He may seek even to work as a doctor, as he had done before, and so he will entrance the individual with whom he has built a rapport, with whom he has gained some consent to work. He would seek to heal in the ethers of those individuals who have physical problems. There are many wonders which have been seen where healing has occurred in the ethers and then in the physical body of an individual.

We would neither condemn this nor would we applaud it, we would simply say that where there is an attempt to bring peace and harmony, then it is working within the Laws of the Universe and of God.

However, if we consider healing in the true Cosmic sense, healing relates to the bringing of wholeness and completeness, and any healing which occurs within an individual has to come from their soul growth. There is always the danger that much which is considered to be healing, is in effect not truly healing. It is rather a repairing operation which can be very temporary because unless there has been growth in the soul and deep and profound learning, then the condition will and must return, for it still has to produce the frequency alteration in the individual enabling them to move into a new consciousness. When this occurs, then there is a return to integration and to wholeness.

This is true healing.

We do not condemn or judge. We observe the truth as we see it here, and many of those who are involved in healing through trance or indeed any state of being, are doing work which is very noble and often very profound.

But nonetheless, the only true healing which can occur is through soul growth and the transmuting of lower energies into higher energies. This will take place when there is learning and understanding. And this cannot be facilitated by another entity. It can be supported, it can be encouraged, but healing can only manifest through the willingness of the Light of the Christ within the heart of the one who is diseased, and his willingness to change and grow."

Q — *'When does the spirit enter the foetus?'*

"When an incarnation is planned, (and it is always planned, both by the entity who seeks to incarnate and also by those who will be touched one way or another intimately by the quality and experience of that incarnation — those who are to be parents, brothers and sisters, close friends and even spiritual mentors who will exist not in the earth plane but perhaps in the ethers or upon the Astral plane or even beyond) and when a decision is reached as to the most appropriate and suitable physical vehicle for a certain out-working of experience, then the soul, at the point of conception, will make its first contact with the physical form, and it will make the contact with the physical form of the foetus in such a manner as to imprint upon it that data and information which is most appropriate for the subsequent development of the physical form.

This process of building in earth time extends to anything up to a period of nine months. Whilst the development of the physical home is under way, the soul will make an attachment to it, but it does not usually make a complete attachment. It is rather a connection which you can best understand as that of a caring parent who would oversee the growth of its child. Thus the soul will monitor the development of the foetus as it expands and grows.

As the time is reached when the actual birth process is beginning to take place, then the soul will make its most permanent attachment, that it might oversee the movement of the physical form from the womb of the mother into the space of the earth's ethers, where it must immediately work with its own etheric form to sustain itself and its life.

Very often the soul, which is the individualised spiritual form, does not make a more permanent connection until days and sometimes hours before the birth occurs into the physical realm. When the baby has entered into the physical dimension, the soul continues to withdraw for long periods of time even when the baby will appear to be awake and conscious. This is because the attachment of the soul and all the vehicles of light to the physical form do not become permanent all at once.

Over the first 21 years there is a growth of the physical and etheric self, there is a growth and attachment of the emotional self and then there is the evolution and attachment of the mental self. In general terms this is not completed until the age of 21, and then the soul is in the position to work through this entity, to learn and discover and to gain the experience which is necessary for its evolution.

Therefore, from our understanding, we can say that the attachment of the soul, or spirit if you wish, to the physical form does not take on a permanent and dynamic relationship until shortly before birth.

There are occasions where, because of the strength of karmic need, a miscarriage, as you would call it, occurs. The entity would stay close to the being through whom he had been elected to come in the possibility that another conception will take place and thus the entity might enter in that fashion."

Q — *'When a channel, such as the channel which you use, goes into a trance state, what happens to his soul or his spirit during that time?'*

"During the state which you refer to as a 'trance state' here is a blending of consciousness.

When we speak through the channel, we use his own mind and his own faculties. The voice which we use is his own voice. It may not be the voice which you are accustomed to, but it is nonetheless a voice which he could and has used in past times, and thus, when we come to work with him, there is a sharing of consciousness.

He removes himself as he would in meditation, into a level of his own mind, which is very much that of the mental body, and we then assume a blending of our own minds with him, and govern the function of his nervous system, and are able to control his speech and the nature of that which is spoken to you.

When this is done his own soul is still very much overseeing that which occurs. Nothing would be permissible which his own soul did not deem to be for his good and in his best interests. There again, this is an arrangement which was made before he incarnated, it is a part of his purpose. He was prepared before he came.

His soul is detached only in the sense that it is overseeing matters, but it is a blending of minds which takes place, and whilst he is no longer in conscious control of his physical organism, he is then engaged in an experience which is rather like meditation. When he returns it will be just as if he has closed his eyes for a few seconds. As you know, when you leave the physical plane, you leave the concept of time and there is no time for him now. For him there appears to be just a short and very brief departure and then he will return."

Q — *'Did Judas' betrayal of Jesus cause his death?'*

"Judas did not and could not harm the Master Jesus, and therefore, it is somewhat of an illusion to suggest that harm was done.

Of course in human terms, He was to suffer pain, but you must also understand that in your life, if there is to be harm inflicted upon you, then that harm is accepted by the one who is harmed.

If you experience physical difficulty as a result of conflict with another, then at some deep level of your being, through the mind of the soul, you have agreed to that particular harm being inflicted upon your physical form. Where this occurs then it can be inflicted by any soul at any level of evolution.

As far as we are concerned we can see no reason why Judas Iscariot needed to be a soul of lesser or greater evolution than the Master Jesus.

Remember that you are speaking of two consciousnesses which are quite independent. The Master Jesus had particular karma which had to be resolved, and this was placed within the relationship of Judas.

The Christ had no karma and therefore, it was the expression of the Christ in the Master Jesus which overcame the situation. However evolved the soul of Judas would have been, he could in no way harm the Master Jesus in the true sense of that idea. He could only impede his evolution, perhaps very briefly, but because of the power within Jesus, he was able to transmute the attempted desecration of his physical temple very quickly, and produce the flowering of the Christ, as was understood in the resurrection.

Judas of himself was a soul of considerable evolution. Having said all that we have said to you, he was a soul of much fine purpose, but because he chose to work within a certain pattern of destiny, whether he was of high or low evolution was of no consequence within the act which was perpetuated.

There are many who would find it extremely glamorous to think that Judas would have to have been a highly evolved soul to perform this action he did, but this is not especially so."

Q — *'I have been reading that Jesus lived long after the crucifixion, and that he did not die on the cross but lived to the age of 70 or so?'*

"The man Jesus, who was born to learn to become the true expression of the Christ Mind upon the earth, was completely imbued with the Christ power when He was baptised by His cousin in the waters of the River Jordan.

When He was baptised, there came a completion of the

process of purification, and the vibration of the Cosmic Christ was able to fuse completely with the physical reality of the man Jesus.

When the crucifixion took place there was no death in the sense that you would understand it here. There was a death of the man Jesus in as much as all the human frailty which was attached to Him fell away from Him, as he realised that He and the Christ Light were one.

When this happened there was an alteration in the vibrational frequency of the body of the man Jesus, and the body of the resurrection manifested. This was not the same as the body of the life before, although it appeared to many to be just such a physical bodies, and they were able to touch that body and feel it. It was nonetheless of a different vibration and a different frequency.

When Jesus, imbued with the pure Christ Light, had undergone His initiation, which occurred on the cross, He came back into the earth consciousness. But as far as those who were there were concerned, He returned to the earth consciousness and walked amongst them for a time to prepare the way for the coming of the Christ Spirit into all men in a manner which they could comprehend.

This of course was the nature of the time you call 'Whitsun', which was Pentecost.

It is really the unfolding of an extra dimension of consciousness within humanity, for Jesus, when imbued with the Christ, had built a new thought pattern through which Man could operate, and he had to leave the final provisions for the expression and development of that thought pattern upon and around the earth. This was through the proof of His continuation, as was revealed to His apostles and those who saw Him in his resurrection body. When He did work thus, he was demonstrating clearly the continuance of life and the infinity of the spirit. Remember that He did that within a society which largely did not understand or believe in the continuation of the spirit after death.

When this was complete the Christ withdrew from the earth sphere into the ethers and Solar Consciousness. And this is the concept of the Ascension. This was the end of the life of the man Jesus upon this physical plane.

However, the Christ poured its Spirit into every atom of the earth through the dropping of the symbolic blood and water upon the ground when His body was pierced. Thus it is that the Christ, and in fact a part of the vibration of the man Jesus as the Christ, remained forever in and with the earth in its most dense vibration.

The man Jesus left the earth and did not continue for a further period in the way which is often suggested by others."

Q — *'What do you think about so called 'Mercy Killing' when people who are terminally ill ask for help to commit suicide ?'*

"You ask in relation to those whose physical condition appears to be terminal and where they seek to make the passing quickly and would therefore ask for the intervention of a third party to administer either drugs or indeed perhaps withdraw medication, that the passing may be obtained more quickly from the physical life into the Astral life and then beyond? Is that indeed the nature of your question?

As we consider the ideas and the principles involved, we would say to you this.

When you finally leave the earth, there is a release on the part of the individual, of all the experience which has gone before, with the key to passing from this life into a new consciousness.

The point which you call death really is based upon the willingness of the personality to free itself from all the emotional and sometimes painful connections you have with this particular incarnation. There follows the release of the higher self into a freer expression of its own identity, and a resolving, very quickly, of some of the karmic understanding at the moment of passing — where you are in relation to those you leave behind in the earth plane and also where you are in relation to those who have gone before you.

For example, it is quite possible and usual for an individual to have very strong emotional connections with those who are still upon the earth and to not have resolved them sufficiently to leave the relationship in physical terms very easily.

It is equally possible that a soul who finds the time for his passing is apparent, could equally be aware of emotional connections with those who have already moved into the Astral life and beyond. He is still, in relation to them, unresolved on many issues as a result of the relationships which unfolded whilst they were on the earth together.

The key to all passing at this time is to obtain the peace which will enable the energy to flow which will break the link and set the soul and its other bodies free from the physical body. This can only truly be so where there is a sufficient degree of relinquishing and acceptance of the experience of the human life which has gone before, and the recognition of its teaching in the next plane and beyond. And when, at the deeper level, the soul is able to come to this understanding with the personality, then the movement from this physical life into the next plane becomes an easier operation.

This is where 'the peace which passes all understanding' descends upon the personality or the lower ego of the individual who is in the terminal illness, as you call it, and enables that soul to direct the transition from the earth into the next life.

The problem with that which is called 'Mercy Killing' is that in certain respects it is no 'mercy'. It can be an illusion that we are helping those to pass who would seek to do so, for it is only when there is some karmic resolution in the area of contact between the soul or the higher self and the personality in respect of that particular incarnation, that sufficient Grace can be achieved, and the energies thus built around the individual will bring the natural flow of the focus of consciousness from this physical life into the next phase of awareness.

Where there is intervention there is always the danger that the entity can arrive in the next plane in a state of confusion and even shock because there could be a rupturing of the connection between the physical and the spiritual life. They may be confused and even unhappy when they have made the transition.

They are able to look back upon the circumstances which enabled the transition to take place and then realise with a clearer and more expansive vision that at a deeper level of their mind there was unfinished business which they had not resolved within their consciousness and therefore they lost an opportunity at the point of their death.

There is, of course, great compassion in the hearts of many who would seek to take away the pain and free a soul from suffering. But it is for him to stay and to learn to free himself through the alteration in his thinking and his relationship with all that has happened during his time here.

We would also say here that were we are able to give sufficient pure healing love which comes from the heart through our hands and our being to those who are near the transition, this healing of course would facilitate the passing and enable them to make the adjustments that they might more easily slip gently away into the next consciousness.

Where those who are termed 'Spiritual healers' have been allowed to work with those in the last stages of their lives, often the passing comes more quickly because of the energies they are able to transmit to the patient. This enables them to be healed at the deeper level of their life to bring this relationship between the soul and the personality to a point and very important resolution, and thus the release may be made into the higher life with greater ease and dignity.

It is understandable that compassion would drive individuals to seek to be involved in what is called 'mercy killing'. But within the terms of the laws of life it is nonetheless an inappropriate thing to do.''

HEARTSTAR RECORDINGS

The following channelled audio cassettes are now available:

"INVOCATION" — A powerful repeat recording of a chant given through Paul whilst in an altered state which can have a profound effect upon consciousness. The recording engineer was puzzled by the reverberations which continued to show on his monitor when the chant had finished and there was no sound audible. To be used in the stillness when free from distractions.   [Ref.: HEARTSTAR 1]

"CHANGES AND SPIRITUAL MAN" — A lecture on Man's nature and the changes before humanity, given in London at the S.A.G.B., 9th. September, 1992. There are also the answers to some questions asked by the audience.   [Ref.: HEARTSTAR 2]

"ASTRAL PLANE CHANGES AND THE COMING HUMAN REDEMPTION" — This lecture was channelled by Paul in Herne Bay, Kent, giving insights into the current changes occurring on the emotional or Astral plane and how they are effecting Mankind.
[Ref.: HEARTSTAR 3]

Further recordings will be made available from October 1993, including Paul's first channelled video cassette "THE LIGHT OF THE SOUL", and all are available from Jacobeus cassettes at the address below.

For details of Heartstar workshops, private channelled sessions and Paul Lambillion's other cassette recordings and books, send an S.A.E. to:

"Workshops / Cassettes / Appointments"
120 Appledown Drive
Bury St. Edmunds
Suffolk   IP32 7HQ
UK